Religion and the Moral Standards of American Businessmen

JOHN W. CLARK, S. J.
College of Business Administration
Loyola University of Los Angeles

SOUTH-WESTERN PUBLISHING CO.

Cincinnati   Chicago   New Rochelle, N. Y.   Dallas
Burlingame, Calif.

TABLE OF CONTENTS

Page

PART I: RELIGIOUS SOURCES OF AMERICAN BUSINESS ETHICS

Chapter

iii

Chapter Page

iv

LIST OF EXHIBITS

EDITOR'S SERIES

We are proud to present in the Editor's Series books that we feel should be available to the profession.

Books in this series are selected and published because of their scholarly nature, their contribution to advanced thinking and research, or their general professional contribution to the improvement of business and economic education. Appropriate manuscripts will be considered on their merit.

Books of the Editor's Series are those that every professionally minded person will want to possess. They should be in every library. Most of them will be useful as supplemental readings for students.

INTRODUCTION

Recent years have witnessed an intensified interest in the subject of business ethics. Professional groups have established committees to formulate codes of conduct and business creeds embodying acceptable norms of business behavior. Under the direction of former Secretary of Commerce, Luther Hodges, a Business Ethics Advisory Council, including some of the most prominent names in American industry, has been formed and has published A Statement on Business Ethics and a Call for Action. Numerous articles and books have explored a great variety of aspects of this subject.

This recent interest in the area of business ethics is not a surprising phenomenon. It is a basic characteristic of every society to seek some rules of conduct which will translate its ideals into concrete expressions in the order of everyday living. As Julian Sorell Huxley has said:

> Every society, in every age, needs some system of beliefs, including a basic attitude to life, an organized set of ideas round which emotion and purpose may gather, and a conception of human destiny. It needs a philosophy and a faith to achieve a guide to orderly living — in other words, a morality. [1]

And morality, if it is to be effective, must be applicable to those areas of activity deemed significant by society.

Growing interest in business ethics reflects a growing appreciation of the role of business in American culture, which in itself is a rather unique phenomenon in the history of Western civilization. [2] For almost the first time in

---

[1] Julian Sorell Huxley, New Bottles for New Wine (London: Chatto and Windus, 1957), p. 245.

[2] Miriam Beard, A History of the Businessman (New York: The Macmillan Company, 1938), p. 1.

history, the businessman is in a position to shape the course of progress in his culture, not merely as a behind-the-scenes influence but as a public figure. The image of the businessman has risen to such a stature that, as one author has put it, he now can for the first time take the role of a true hero in the popular mind.[3] The awakening of a sense of business ethics is part of this new appreciation of the businessman. And it likewise marks a significant step in self-awareness, as it is businessmen themselves who are providing much of the impetus in this effort to find a deeper understanding of the meaning of moral and ethical conduct.

But while much of the literature about business ethics now being published is of great value, there exists a certain dearth of theoretical material relating to this field. Many of the popular books and articles now available draw heavily on the experience of their authors and embody their own personal convictions and attitudes towards the various dimensions of the subject. Few attempts have been made to trace the sources of American business values or to determine what the actual standards of businessmen are. This present work makes an effort in each of these directions. First, it attempts to explore the religious influence on the formation of American business mores. Then it attempts to appraise the actual moral standards of contemporary leaders in the business world.

In discussing the religious influence on business standards, a deliberate effort has been made to avoid a detailed collection of precepts relating to specific business practices. Instead of describing the influence of religious creeds by an extensive examination of their moral codes, what has been aimed for is an understanding of the broad spirit of the major religious faiths as they have had an impact on the course of business morality. Thus specific directives and imperatives of individual religious groups are introduced only as explicative or illustrative of the basic orientation they contribute to an appreciation of the business world. The object of the study is not a

---

[3]Joseph W. McGuire, Business and Society (New York: McGraw-Hill Book Co., Inc., 1963), pp. 201-205.

viii

comprehensive presentation of the moral content of these faiths, but rather an understanding of their influence in the formation of the businessman's basic attitude towards the problems of ethical behavior in business circumstances.

In the second part of the present study an effort is made to sound the parameters of the actual moral content of contemporary businessmen. Empirical tools have been used to study the area of agreement and disagreement in the moral convictions of a group of executives. It is important to note that the study makes no attempt to investigate the conduct of participants in the study. It simply explores the question of what the moral standards of these men are. It deliberately excludes the further question of how faithfully these executives translate their beliefs into the concrete dimensions of their day-to-day decisions. By so doing, it was felt that a more candid expression of ethical conviction could be obtained than if the participants were also asked to make some kind of examination of conscience into their personal conformity to their standards.

The study concludes with an attempt to distill from both parts of the previous investigations some general norms which might be judged as common to the ethical mores of most American businessmen. These are proposed as guides which might serve as the foundation for the development of a true business ethic which can become the premise for further studies and investigations in this important area. If it does this with a certain degree of objectivity, it will make a definite contribution to a growing field of knowledge which is of vital interest to the business community, and indeed, to American society as well.

ACKNOWLEDGMENTS

The author wishes to acknowledge his gratitude and appreciation to a number of men who have contributed substantially to the present effort. Professor Cyril J. O'Donnell of the University of California (Los Angeles) first turned the attention of the writer to the area of business ethics and generously gave guidance, direction, and encouragement throughout the preparation of this manuscript. Dr. Harold Kasarjian, also of UCLA, provided close support through the empirical phase of the study. His sense of scholarship, technical competence, and enthusiasm in the search for truth have been of immeasurable help to the author. Dr. Melville Dalton, also of UCLA, has made valuable comments and criticisms through the whole text. Dean Wilbur R. Garrett and Dr. John C. Haggart of Loyola University of Los Angeles and Dr. Anelise Mosich of University of Southern California have offered encouragement and valuable advice. In addition, any author is acutely aware that his own thought has been developed through the collective influence of a number of authors and teachers in the area of his interests. Wherever possible, explicit acknowledgment is given to these sources; nevertheless, the present insights and convictions of a researcher often find their sources in his readings and studies of the past. To all these men, the author extends his gratitude and appreciation. Any errors or deficiencies in the study are, of course, the sole responsibility of the present writer.

John W. Clark, S. J.

Chapter 1

THE SOURCES OF AMERICAN BUSINESS ETHICS: PROTESTANT INFLUENCES

INTRODUCTION

THE AMERICAN CULTURAL MIX

The United States in many respects possesses one of the most heterogenic cultures of modern times. Not only did English, Dutch, German, Swede, Welsh, and French colonists bring to its shores the customs and traditions of their native lands, but they also brought with them a number of new ideas which were sweeping European capitals of their day.[1] The literature and art of the Renaissance, the science of Newton and Descartes, the "New Philosophy" of the seventeenth and eighteenth centuries, the broad currents of intellectual revival known as the Enlightenment, and the diverse religious commitments of the early colonists all contributed to the cultural "mix" which uniquely characterized early America.[2]

To weigh each of these influences in an effort to assay their impact on contemporary business morals would be a complex task and one beyond the scope of the present limited effort. Nevertheless, some appreciation of the ethical heritage of the American businessman seems fundamental to an understanding of his present condition. Accordingly, this chapter investigates in broad outline the impact of one of the most strategic parameters in the development of American business morals: the religious influence.

---

[1] This idea is developed at length by Merle Curti, The Growth of American Thought (New York: Harper and Brothers, 1943), pp. 3-24.

[2] Ralph Barton Perry, Characteristically American (New York: A. A. Knopf Co., 1949), pp. 6-7.

THE RELIGIOUS FACTOR IN AMERICAN MORALS

The choice of a religious factor as important in the formation of American business morals reflects to a certain degree the judgment of the present researcher. However, this judgment is by no means singular. Ralph Barton Perry has observed that the religious commitments of Americans have had a profound influence on their whole cultural development:

> The general Hebraic-Christian-Biblical tradition embraces ideas so familiar that, like the air, they are inhaled without effort or attention. And where, as in America, this theistic belief is traditional and pervasive, it determines disbelief as well as belief. . . . Theism in the broad Hebraic-Christian-Biblical sense is in Americans the norm of both fidelity and infidelity. [3]

And where such an influence affects the whole society, the business community could hardly avoid its impact.

Protestantism undoubtedly represents the most significant religious influence on American mores. Indeed, its influence exceeds the proportion of Protestants among the American population. For while in 1963 Catholicism was the faith of approximately 25 percent of Americans, [4] its influence in the development of American morals has been less than these figures lead one to suspect. Except for Maryland, the colonials were for the most part strongly moulded by the Protestant tradition, especially in Puritan and evangelical Protestantism. The Catholicism of the later immigrants came to American shores only after the main traits of the American character were formed. Further, Catholicism as a rule did not reach the upper economic, political, and cultural levels of American society until a relatively recent date. [5] Much of Catholic social interest has centered on the labor movement and the concept of social justice. A number of Catholic scholars, such as Msgr.

---

[3] Ibid., pp. 93-94.

[4] Statistical Abstract of the United States: 1963 (Washington, D.C.: U.S. Government Printing Office, 1963), pp. 19, 48.

[5] Perry, op. cit., p. 7.

John A. Ryan, Msgr. John F. Cronin, and Bishop Francis Haas, have made important contributions to the American Labor Movement; but their writings have been relatively recent and have pertained to only a limited aspect of total American ethical milieu.

To a degree, the same observation can be made of the Jewish faith. Not only were the first Jewish immigrants members of a minority group in colonial America, but they were also members of a group which had been discriminated against through centuries of Christian history. In America the Jews suffered discrimination similar to that which they had received in Europe, and such discrimination evoked in them something of a mistrust of the majority and an aloofness from the majority's cultural activities. Such discrimination also tightened the internal cohesion of the Jewish community, and no doubt is partly accountable for the fact that Jewish cultural values, like Catholic values, were not early assimilated into the American character.[6]

Thus, as William Hollingsworth Whyte has observed:

> Officially, we are a people who hold to the Protestant Ethic. Because of the denominational implications of the term many would deny its relevance to them, but let them eulogize the American Dream, however, and they virtually define the Protestant Ethic. Whatever the embroidery, there is almost always the thought that pursuit of individual salvation through hard work, thrift, and competitive struggle is the heart of the American achievement.[7]

SCOPE OF THE PRESENT CHAPTER

This chapter explores the influence of the Protestant ethic on American business. It is not an empirical study. No attempt here is made to quantify this influence, to determine in the concrete its relative significance vis-à-vis other determinants of American mores. Rather, what is aimed for is an understanding of the sources of some of the

---

[6]C. Bezalel Sherman, The Jew Within American Society (Detroit: Wayne State University Press, 1961), p. 58.

[7]William H. Whyte, Jr., The Organization Man (New York: Simon and Schuster. 1956), p. 4.

values of businessmen and an appreciation of how these values have been interpreted through three critical phases of American history.

THEORETICAL ORIGINS OF THE PROTESTANT ETHIC: THE WEBERIAN THESIS

THE SPIRIT OF CAPITALISM

Undoubtedly the most famous work on the relationship between Protestantism and the conduct of businessmen has been the two essays of Max Weber, written in 1904 and 1905. Subsequently translated into English and published in a single volume in 1930, The Protestant Ethic and the Spirit of Capitalism has conditioned every discussion of this topic since that time. Though we are looking to the standards rather than the conduct of businessmen, Weber's work is a convenient place to begin the present investigation.

Capitalism, as Weber sees it, is more than a modern adaptation of the perennial acquisitive spirit. It is the pursuit of profit in a new and unprecedented way: "by means of continuous, rational organization of formally free labor."[8] Thus it implies not just a more systematic approach to acquisitiveness; it implies a new kind of approach. While formerly the pursuit of riches was regarded at best as something of a personal inclination which was ethically neutral, the spirit of capitalism looks upon such endeavor as a moral duty:

>   According to this philosophy, if a man is rich, he has himself to thank; if he is destitute, he has himself to blame. The rich man is an object of commendation, and not merely of envy; to be a pauper is not a misfortune, but a disgrace. When an individual possesses the qualities of austerity, reliability, energy, industry, self-control, marital fidelity, frugality, sobriety, thrift, self-reliance, and foresight, the

---

[8]Max Weber, The Protestant Ethic and the Spirit of Capitalism (New York: Charles Scribner's Sons, 1952), pp. 16, 21.

effect is wealth. When, on the other hand, a man is pleasure-loving, untrustworthy, sluggish, idle, dissipated, irregular, extravagant, frivolous, wasteful, dependent, and careless, the effect is poverty. The effect, being traced to its cause, is to be dealt with accordingly.[9]

This spirit of capitalism contrasts significantly with the ideals of pre-Reformation Christianity, i. e. , Catholicism. For Catholic preachers tended to frown upon the rich, extol the virtue of poverty, and with an emphasis on "unworldly" asceticism, to regard occupation with the material as inferior to purely intellectual pursuits. How then was the spirit of capitalism able to overcome the somewhat hostile attitude of Catholicism?

LUTHER'S DOCTRINE OF THE "CALLING"

To answer this question Weber turns to a consideration of the religious doctrine of the sixteenth-century reformers. As a result of his doctrine of salvation by faith alone, Luther opposed the Catholic doctrine of meritorious good works, and especially rejected the Catholic ideals of the ascetic and monastic life. In his effort to return to the spirit of early Christianity, he was profoundly influenced by the eschatological spirit of the first-century Christians: since everyone was simply waiting for the second coming of Christ, and with it the end of the world, there was no need to become too concerned with external works. Luther recommended that the faithful remain in the stations and in the worldly occupations they were in, for one could obtain salvation in any walk of life; and in the short time which remained to them, what counted was their faith, not their works.[10]

As Luther's thought reached greater maturity through his involvement in political and other practical affairs, his doctrine of the "calling" underwent a subtle change: it became identical with the idea of complete abandonment to

---

[9]Ralph Barton Perry, Puritanism and Democracy (New York: The Vanguard Press, 1944), p. 302.

[10]Weber, op. cit. , p. 84.

the divine will in the absolute acceptance of things as they were.[11]   Historical events became manifestations of the Providence of God, to be accepted with faith, but not to be tampered with. Thus Luther saw a more and more intimate connection between worldly affairs and the Providence of God. Each Christian's duty was to accept his involvement in worldly affairs as his calling. And his perfection consisted not in choosing the more noble occupations, but rather in accepting the occupation determined for him by Providence.

JOHN CALVIN'S CONTRIBUTION: THE MORAL ATHLETE

Luther's doctrine of the "calling" in some respects leads away from the justification of business activity; he saw such activity as something quite irrelevant to the main current of life. But in the hands of another reformer, John Calvin, the doctrine of the "calling" took on a new dimension, and worldly involvement was elevated from the realm of the insignificant to the realm of the sacred. Calvin accepted Luther's doctrine of salvation by faith alone but grappled more directly with the dogma of predestination. For Calvin saw that if good works were of no avail, and if one were saved by faith alone, which was a free gift of God which no one could merit, then salvation was wholly up to God. Some, God destined to have faith, and these were the elect. Others were not so fortunate; they were predestined to be damned.

In such a scheme of things, the individual Christian had more than idle curiosity about whether he personally was among the predestined elect or damned.   There were several counsels to set the troubled soul at rest. First, the Christian should feel himself absolutely certain of his salvation since any lack of self-confidence was due to insufficient grace and suggestive of reprobation. Secondly, the Christian was exhorted to absorb himself in worldly affairs, and this for two reasons: because he would in this way take his mind off his doubts about personal salvation, and also because he would be fulfilling the will of God according to the Lutheran concept of the "calling." Indeed,

---

[11]Ibid. , p. 85.

by the fruits of his own life, the Calvinist could recognize his own election. Good works, austerity, frugality, and industry became indispensable, not as the means of winning salvation, but as the signs of election. They were the sure way to dispose of the fear of damnation. [12]

Thus by an extraordinarily subtle line of reasoning, the most "other-worldly" of the Protestant faiths baptized the activities which characterized the worldly, sixteenth-century entrepreneur. What formerly had been looked upon as a base, or at best, a morally neutral activity became a means of fulfilling one's divine "calling," of perfectly abandoning oneself to the divine Providence, of manifesting in one's own person incontestable signs of predestination.

To be sure, there was at this stage still an incompatibility between Calvinism and wealth. But this incompatibility was soon reconciled by the doctrine of stewardship: the wealthy man possesses his riches not for his own benefit, but for society. The Calvinist with this doctrine of stewardship found himself remarkably at home in the business world. The qualities which characterized business success he saw as certain signs of divine election. The wealth which was the natural outcome of industry and frugality was at least accepted, if not enjoyed. For God gave to the religious man the responsibility of being steward of the goods of the earth. Like a king of divine right, he was to administer this wealth for the benefit of all, but for his stewardship he was responsible to God alone. And at all costs the Calvinist was warned to shield himself from the dangers of wealth: pride, sensuality, and luxury. This could be done by an unswerving fidelity to the virtues of the moral athlete: austerity, frugality, industry, and thrift.

THE PROTESTANT ETHIC IN AMERICA

Of particular interest to the work of these pages is the impact of this Protestant ethic among American businessmen. The following historical investigation is not meant to be exhaustive, but rather to exhibit the Protestant ethic as a moral code which influenced business practices through

---

[12]Ibid., p. 114.

three critical periods in American history: (1) the colonial period, (2) the period of the "Triumph of Capitalism,"[13] and (3) the contemporary period.

THE COLONIAL PERIOD

The influence of the Reformation came to American shores with several religious sects, but it is chiefly the Puritans of New England who implanted the qualities of the moral athlete in New World soil. To be sure, it has been suggested that the Puritans were far from the predestinarian Calvinists they are sometimes made out to be,[14] but even a cursory study of their history points to the qualities we have attributed above to the moral athlete. Today there is considerable disagreement among scholars whether the influence of Puritanism has been for good or ill,[15] but there is hardly a reputable historian who will question the assertion that it has been one of the principal influences in the development of the American character. As Ralph Barton Perry has observed:

> The Puritans imprinted on English and American institutions a quality of manly courage, self-reliance, and sobriety. We are still drawing on the reserves of spiritual vigor which they accumulated.[16]

It is natural to begin here the investigation of the Protestant ethic in America.

Cotton Mather. Among the voices of Puritanism, few are more famous than that of Cotton Mather. A prominent Puritan divine who was regarded as one of the most forceful and influential preachers of his time, Mather, in his works, covers a wide field of theological speculation as he

---

[13]Louis B. Hacker, The Triumph of American Capitalism (New York: Simon and Schuster, 1940), 460 pp.

[14]Samuel Eliot Morison, The Puritan Pronaos (New York: New York University Press, 1936), p. 10.

[15]George M. Waller (ed.), Puritanism in Early America (Boston: D. C. Heath and Company, 1950), p. v.

[16]Perry, Puritanism and Democracy, p. 268.

delved into such widely divergent subjects as the perplexing problem of predestination and the puzzling, enigmatic questions of diabolic possession and witch-burning. It is his observations on the relation of business and religion which are of particular interest here.

Mather most specifically deals with the application of religious teaching to business practice in Two Brief Discourses, One Directing a Christian in His General Calling; Another Directing Him in His Personal Calling, a small work published in Boston in 1701. Besides the general calling which each Christian has "to serve the Lord Jesus Christ," each Christian also has a "personal calling," a particular employment by which he is useful to the community in which he lives. As Mather puts it:

> A Christian at his two callings is a man in a boat, rowing for heaven, the house which our heavenly father has intended for us. If he mind but one of his callings, be it which it will, he pulls the oar, but on one side of the boat, and will but make a poor dispatch to the shore of eternal blessedness.[17]

It is not enough to pray; the servant of God must also be occupied about:

> some settled business, wherein a Christian should for the most part spend most of his time and this, so that he may glorify God, by doing good for others, and getting of Good for himself.[18]

Mather spells out in detail the relationship of business to religion in a somewhat lengthy passage which reveals the baptism of business activity by the Protestant ethic:

> Would a man rise in business? I say, then let him rise in business. It was foretold (Proverbs 22.29), "Seest thou a man diligent in his business? He shall stand before kings." He shall come to

---

[17]Cotton Mather, Two Brief Discourses, One Directing a Christian in His General Calling; Another Directing Him in His Personal Calling. Quotations of this work are from A. Whitney Griswold, "Three Puritans on Prosperity," The New England Quarterly, VII (September, 1934), 475-88. The present quote is from p. 479.

[18]Loc. cit.

preferment. And it was instanced by him who fore-
told it (I Kings 11.28), "Solomon, seeing that the
young man was industrious, he made him a ruler." I
tell you, with diligence a man may do marvelous
things. Young man, work hard while you are young.
You'll reap the effects of it when you are old. Yea,
how can you ordinarily enjoy any rest at night if you
have not been well at work in the day? Let your business engross most of your time. [19]

Let every man have the discretion to be well instructed in, and well acquainted with, all the mys-
teries of his occupation. Be master of your trade;
count it a disgrace to be no workman. [20]

In such a way God rallied to the cause of the Puritan businessman, and as he practiced Christian virtues in his
worldly calling, God crowned his efforts with material success. "All the day our business will go on the better, all
the day for your thus being faithful to God." [21]

To be sure, Cotton Mather often excoriated businessmen for leaning too heavily on the oar of their personal
calling, emphasizing the acquisition of wealth at the cost of
honesty, piety, temperance, and sobriety. There was more
than one way of steering their boat away from the shore of
eternal blessedness. Yet in Mather we find almost a perfect reflection of the doctrine of Calvin, so perfect that it
has led one notable historian to conclude:

Cotton Mather did not invent this doctrine: he
merely gave it expression. His utterances are of interest to us not so much for the persuasive influence
they had on his contemporaries, as because they represent the mind of orthodox Puritanism two centuries
ago. They indicate that thinking men were casting
about in their minds for a moral sanction for money-
making, and that they found that salvation in the ethical system proposed by Martin Luther and John
Calvin. Thus, in a sense, Cotton Mather deserves

---

[19] Griswold, op. cit., pp. 479-80.

[20] Ibid., p. 480.

[21] Loc. cit.

recognition as one of the first to teach American business men to serve God by making money. [22]

Benjamin Franklin. If Cotton Mather was foremost among the Puritan preachers of his day, it was another Puritan, a man of affairs, who became the foremost champion and popularizer of the Protestant ethic on American shores. Benjamin Franklin was born five years after Mather published his Two Brief Discourses, and was so profoundly influenced by the spirited New England divine that he later acknowledged his indebtedness in a letter to Cotton Mather's son. [23] Undoubtedly the ministers of Puritanism were gladdened to find such an eloquent and popular champion of their moral creed, even though by middle age Franklin had abandoned the faith of his father for a more comfortable approach to God.

Franklin's testimony in support of the Protestant ethic abounds through the twelve volumes of his works, though it is obvious that he is more oriented to the practical than to the theological speculation. In his autobiography he mentions the thirteen virtues which he made the subject of a daily review. The list reads like a muster of the economic virtues: temperance, silence, order, resolution, frugality, sincerity, justice, moderation, cleanliness, tranquility, chastity, and humility. [24] In 1748 in a letter to a friend, he expresses his own conviction of the relationship between economic success and the virtues of the moral athlete;

> In short, the way to wealth, if you desire it, is as plain as the way to market. It depends chiefly on two words, industry and frugality--that is, waste neither time nor money, but make the best use of both. With industry and frugality nothing will do, and with them everything. He that gets all he can honestly, and saves all he gets (necessary expenses excepted), will certainly become rich, if that Being who governs

---

[22] Griswold, op. cit., p. 483.

[23] Charles L. Sanford (ed.), Benjamin Franklin and the American Character (Boston: D. C. Heath and Co., 1956), p. 45.

[24] John Bigelow (ed.), The Works of Benjamin Franklin, Federal Edition, Vol. I (New York: G. Putnam's Sons, 1904), pp. 189-92.

the world, to whom all should look for a blessing on their honest endeavors, does not, in his wise providence, otherwise determine. [25]

It was especially through his Poor Richard's Almanac that Franklin spread his gospel of getting rich by means of the economic virtues. In 1757 he skimmed through twenty-five of his yearly Almanacs, pulled together the best of Richard's pithy sayings relating to the quest for wealth, and published them separately in a little work which was to become one of his best-known writings: The Way to Wealth. [26] In this small volume, Franklin has Father Abraham pave the way to wealth with four virtues: industry, diligence, frugality, and the blessing of heaven. Some of the proverbs reflect the persistence of the Protestant ethic in the mind of this man who had by this time abandoned Protestantism:

God helps those who help themselves.
Sloth, like rust, consumes faster than labor wears,
    while the used key is always bright.
But dost thou love life, then do not squander time, for
    that is the stuff that life is made of.
Laziness travels so slowly that Poverty soon over-
    takes him.
He that hath a trade, hath an estate, and he that hath
    a calling, hath an office of profit and honor.
Diligence is the mother of good luck, and God gives
    all things to industry.
Plough deep while sluggards sleep, and you will have
    corn to sell and to keep.
Keep thy shop and it will keep thee.
A fat kitchen makes a lean will.
Buy what thou hast no need of and ere long thou shall
    sell thy necessities.
Always taking out of the meal tub and never putting in
    soon comes to the bottom of the meal tub.
Silks and satins, scarlet and velvets, put out the
    kitchen fire. Rather go to bed supperless than
    rise in debt.

---

[25] Ibid., Vol. II, pp. 236-37.

[26] Carl Van Doren, Benjamin Franklin (New York: The Viking Press, 1938), p. 266.

> Do not depend too much on your own industry and
> frugality and prudence, though excellent things,
> they may all be blasted without the blessing of
> heaven. [27]

As has been noted, by the time that Franklin collected
these maxims, he was no longer an orthodox Puritan. Indeed, his revolt against the rigorous creed of his parents
may be somewhat accountable for his acceptability and
popularity among his contemporaries. Yet his conviction
in the principles of the Protestant ethic always remained,
and this strange union of a wavering faith on the speculative
level and an unwavering commitment to an apparently inconsistent moral code on the practical level is typical of
many Americans of both his own and the present age. As
one noted authority has expressed it:

> In his austere moralism, Franklin was undoubt-
> edly a Puritan, however much he may have revolted
> against Calvinism. . . . In other ways Franklin was
> no doubt a typical eighteenth-century man of the
> world, but as a moralist he was a child of the New
> England frontier. [28]

THE AGE OF THE "TRIUMPH OF CAPITALISM"

Important as are beginnings, it is equally important to
see the development of the Protestant ethic in the period
characterized by Louis Hacker as the "Triumph of Capitalism." This was the age in which the American spirit of
free enterprise reached its zenith, and both economic and
ethical creeds were expressed with a candor and simplicity
which appear remarkable today. The period of 1880 to
1914, for all its excesses, is particularly appropriate for
the manifestation of ethical values in the business environment. Two men stand out as embodiments of the moral
attitudes of the period, not because they are typical of their
age, but because they propound a theory almost universally
accepted by businessmen of their time.

---

[27] Bigelow, op. cit. , Vol. II, pp. 26-38, passim.

[28] Herbert Wallace Schneider, The Puritan Mind (New York: H.
Holt and Co. , 1930), pp. 255-56.

William Lawrence. One of the most noteworthy and influential clergymen at the turn of the century was William Lawrence, Protestant Episcopal Bishop of Massachusetts. For over thirty-two years his voice rang out from the pulpit of the Episcopal Cathedral of Boston, and thousands fell under the sway of his flowing rhetoric.

Lawrence best expressed his support of the Protestant ethic in an article originally published in World's Work in 1901: "The Relation of Wealth to Morals." This brilliantly written essay takes to task what Lawrence sees as a Christian distrust of material prosperity. "Christians," he says, "shrink with some foreboding at the great increase of riches, and question whether in the long run material prosperity does not tend toward the disintegration of character." [29] Lawrence takes exception to this popular attitude; for, as he asserts, "Neither history, experience nor the Bible necessarily sustains the common distrust of the effect of material wealth on morality." [30] On the contrary:

> When the question is asked, "Is the material prosperity of this nation favorable or unfavorable to the morality of the people?" I say with all emphasis, "In the long run and by all means favorable!" [31]

The reason for Lawrence's optimism is not long in coming. He sees that Christian virtues practiced well will almost naturally lead to wealth:

> Put two men in adjoining fields, one man strong and normal, the other weak and listless. One picks up his spade, turns over the earth, and works till sunset. The other turns over a few clods, gets a drink from the spring, takes a nap, and loafs back to his work. In a few years one will be rich for his

---

[29] William Lawrence, "The Relation of Wealth to Morals," World's Work, I (January, 1901), 286-92. Reprinted in Gail Kennedy (ed.), Democracy and the Gospel of Wealth (Boston: D. C. Heath and Co., 1949), pp. 68-76. Page references to this work are from the reprint. The immediate reference is to p. 68.

[30] Ibid., p. 69.

[31] Ibid., p. 70.

needs, and the other a pauper dependent on the first, and growling at his prosperity.

Put ten thousand immoral men to live and work in one fertile valley and ten thousand moral men to live and work in the next valley, and the question is soon answered as to who wins the material wealth. Godliness is in league with riches. [32]

Godliness is in league with riches! It is the virtue of industry and hard work which has once again placed the laurel of wealth upon the brow of the Christian. Indeed, barring a few cases of "ephemeral success, which sometimes follows deceit and breeds a body of commercial frauds:"

in the long run, it is only to the man of morality that wealth comes. We believe in the harmony of God's universe. We know that it is only by working along His laws natural and spiritual that we can work with efficiency. Only by working along the lines of right thinking and right living can the secrets and wealth of nature be revealed. We, like the Psalmist, occasionally see the wicked prosper, but only occasionally. [33]

Another important virtue of the Protestant ethic is also contained in the preaching of Bishop Lawrence: wealth is held in stewardship for the good of all:

The fact is that only a small fraction of their [i. e. , the rich] income can be . spent on their own pleasure and luxury; the bulk of what they get has to be reinvested, and becomes the means whereby thousands earn their wages. They are simply trustees of a fraction of the material prosperity. [34]

Lawrence sees the fundamental relationship between wealth and morals as a sound one, and this precisely because the economic virtues of the moral athlete assure

---

[32] Lawrence, op. cit. , p. 69.

[33] Loc. cit.

[34] Lawrence, op. cit. , p. 70.

material success. And material prosperity, in turn, works for the furtherance of Christian virtue:

> Material prosperity is helping to make the national character sweeter, more joyous, more unselfish, more Christlike. That is my answer to the question as to the relation of material prosperity to morality. [35]

Bishop Lawrence, then, gives eloquent testimony to the presence of the Protestant ethic in the religious teaching at the turn of the last century. It will be illuminating to consider its influence in the life of a prominent businessman of the same era.

John D. Rockefeller. Earl Latham has observed that "the American businessman is a symbol of American culture the world around, and for many people that symbol was personified by John D. Rockefeller."[36] Not only does Rockefeller personify the American businessman, he also exemplifies the spirit of the Protestant ethic which was so much a part of the business creed in the latter half of the last century and through the early decades of the present century. Born and raised in a strict Baptist family, young John was steeped in the Calvinistic traditions from his earliest years. As Allan Nevins, his best biographer, tells us:

> His mother had drilled into him the basic virtues of honesty, sobriety, industry, truthfulness and altruism, and had helped give him a fervent religious faith which reinforced his uprightness. . . Both his father and his mother, but particularly the former, had taught him business thrift, foresight and industry.[37]

---

[35]Ibid., p. 73.

[36]Earl Latham (ed.), John D. Rockefeller: Robber Baron or Industrial Statesman? (Boston: D.C. Heath and Co., 1949), p. v.

[37]Allan Nevins, Study in Power: John D. Rockefeller, Industrialist and Philanthropist, 2 vols. (New York: Charles Scribner's Sons, 1953), I, 15.

The young man learned these lessons well, and from his earliest years proved himself frugal, industrious, self-reliant, and dependable. [38]   These same qualities characterized his early business career and marked him among his peers as a man of destiny.   Maurice B. Clark, his first business partner, describes him at the age of twenty: "He was methodical to the extreme, careful as to details and exacting to a fraction.   If there was a cent due us, he wanted it.   If there was a cent due a customer, he wanted the customer to have it. "[39]   This spirit of industry and meticulous care of details represented more than a man bent on business success.   Already in Rockefeller it was more an issue of duty and principle than a path to financial gain.

Though he was generous in his charities, even from an early age the lesson of personal thrift was never forgotten in the management of his business affairs.   One employee has recounted an event which took place in the early 1870's, at a time when Rockefeller, in his mid-thirties, already possessed a sizable fortune:

He [Rockefeller] watched a machine for filling the tin cans.   One dozen cans stood on a wooden platform beneath a dozen pipes.   A man pulled a lever, and each pipe discharged exactly five gallons of kerosene into a can.   Still on a wooden carrier, the dozen cans were pushed along to another machine wherein twelve tops were swiftly clamped fast on the cans.   Thence they were pushed to the last machine in which just enough solder to fasten and seal the lid was dropped on each can.

Mr. Rockefeller listened in silence while an expert told all about the various machines used to save labor and time and expense in the process.   At last Mr. Rockefeller asked:

"How many drops of solder do you use on each can?"

"Forty. "

"Have you ever tried thirty-eight?   No?   Would

---

[38] Ibid. , I, 9.

[39] Ibid. , I, 14.

you mind having some sealed with thirty-eight and let me know?"

Six or seven percent of these cans leaked. Then thirty-nine drops were used. None leaked. It was tried with one hundred, five hundred, a thousand cans. None leaked. Thereafter every can was sealed with thirty-nine drops. [40]

In explaining the significance of this incident, Nevins remarks that "Rockefeller grasped early the great truth that inefficiency and waste are a form of dishonesty, a theft of wealth which might be used for the general good."[41]

Though he was not a stingy man, a letter to his son John Jr., written fifteen years later in 1888, demonstrates the fact that he was never prodigal with his personal expenditures. He writes:

Aunty and I went to the Harlem River with Flash and Midnight in a new cutter which cost $300. Very extravagant I know but the sleighing is so good I could not resist the temptation to buy it and hope to get the worth of our money. [42]

And the same year, while on a trip through Europe, he exhibited this same concern for thrift in his personal expenditures:

Early in this European tour, Rockefeller, finding that the courier he had engaged was cheating him unmercifully, got rid of the man and took on the management of the party himself. He worked like a slave over details. "I can see him now," writes his son, "going over the long French bills, studying each item, many of them being unintelligible to him. "Poulets!" he would exclaim, "What are poulets, John?". . . And so on down the bill. Father was never willing to pay a bill which he did not know to be

---

[40]Nevins, op. cit., I, 280-81. This reputedly saved $2,500 the first year, and "as the export business doubled, quadrupled and sextupled, the saving accumulated into a fund of hundreds of thousands of dollars." (Ibid., I, 428.)

[41]Ibid., I, p. 281.

[42]Nevins, op. cit., II, 83.

correct in all its items. Such care in small things might seem penurious to some people, yet to him it was the working out of a life principle.[43]

And in other respects, too, temperance characterized his life:

> Rockefeller's personal tastes remained for the most part extremely simple. He took no interest in clothes, and though he dressed neatly, his family found difficulty in getting him to renew his suits betimes. . . . At table he always ate sparingly. . . and he inculcated in each child the duty of giving to churches and charities, these gifts being made from earnings.[44]

Nevins, in another passage, describes Rockefeller's attitude toward another characteristic of the Protestant ethic, the stewardship of wealth:

> Rockefeller always regarded himself as a trustee rather than an owner. His statement at the University of Chicago that "God gave me money," sometimes quoted as a piece of sanctimonious arrogance, was actually uttered in a spirit of complete humility. He devoutly believed that Providence had made him a trustee for these hundreds of millions, not to be kept but to be widely disbursed. He meant to see that the gold was used to do the utmost possible good.[45]

There is much controversy today concerning whether Rockefeller was an industrial statesman and organizational genius or a cruel and calculating robber baron. Probably neither judgment is completely true of the man. Like others, he had in him the good and the bad, the noble and the ignoble. But the character and personality of John D. Rockefeller becomes easier to understand when his life is considered in the light of the Protestant ethic.

---

[43] Ibid. , II, 94.

[44] Nevins, op. cit. , II, 86-87.

[45] Ibid. , II, 435.

THE CONTEMPORARY PERIOD

It has been forcefully argued that in recent times the Protestant ethic plays a smaller role in the motivation of economic activity than in times past.[46] Further, the values of the Protestant ethic have been challenged on another score. It is argued that it stands in opposition to the economic spirit most suitable to a consumption-oriented economy — an economy whose success is based upon the prodigality of the population, where frugality can destroy demand and thrift can stifle consumption, and where national prosperity depends upon an abundance of "nonproductive consumers" in the economy.[47]

In spite of such criticism, the Protestant ethic continues to have its defenders and continues to inspire businessmen to the practices of the moral athlete. Two men, one an outstanding theoretician, the other a successful businessman, give witness to the relevance of this creed to the modern world.

Kenneth E. Boulding. One of the prominent economic and social analysts of present-day society, Kenneth E. Boulding, has become an articulate apologist and proponent of the Protestant ethic. Boulding traces its influence not only in the development of the spirit of capitalism, but also in the continued success of the American system as we know it today:

> The thesis of Max Weber and his school that the Protestant Ethic has influenced the development of capitalism is now well accepted. Though one's estimate of the quantitative importance of this influence will depend to a great extent on the interpretation of history which one favors, the direction of the influence can hardly be in doubt.
>
> What has not, I think, been pointed out with sufficient force is that the Protestant Ethic has contributed to the success of capitalistic institutions in

---

[46]Whyte, op. cit., pp. 4-7.

[47]David Riesman, The Lonely Crowd (Garden City, N.Y.: Doubleday, 1953), p. 34. See also: David Morris Potter, People of Plenty (Chicago: University of Chicago Press, 1954), passim.

regard to their fostering a high rate of economic progress. [48]

Boulding sees the Protestant ethic working in a somewhat different way than does Weber. For Boulding, Protestantism reflects a discontent with compromise and attempts to return to the perfection of Christianity in apostolic times. But such perfection is an ideal which almost necessarily falls short of its mark, and then it is that:

> the perfectionist subsides into the Puritan, and groups of people arise practicing, with some success, the minor virtues of thrift, hard work, sobriety, punctuality, honesty, fulfillment of promises, devotion to the family and so on. The minor virtues, however, lead almost inevitably to accumulation and increased productivity, and eventually therefore to an escape from poverty. [49]

It is true, Boulding admits, that the modern world has drifted somewhat away from the Protestant ethic. And yet, the continued success of the capitalistic system and the survival of American prosperity depend upon a reaffirmation and recommitment to what Boulding calls "Protestantism's Lost Economic Gospel," which he describes succinctly and persuasively:

> Poverty is a result of sin, and the eradication of sin through the power of Christ eliminates the cause of poverty. Sin, moreover, is identified with individual behavior, with sloth, drunkenness, licentiousness, untruthfulness and so on. Once the individual is made aware of the power of Christ in his life these vices are progressively, or quite dramatically, eliminated, and no matter how poor he is he starts working and saving and so begins to climb the economic ladder. [50]

---

[48] Kenneth E. Boulding, "Religious Foundations of Economic Progress," Harvard Business Review, III(3) (May-June, 1952), 35.

[49] Ibid., p. 36.

[50] Kenneth E. Boulding, "Our Lost Economic Gospel," The Christian Century, LXVII(33) (August 16, 1950), 970.

But Boulding goes further. He adds a new dimension to the arguments in support of the Protestant ethic. Not only does it hold promise of individual success and personal salvation, but in it Boulding sees the greatest hope for society, especially in underdeveloped countries:

> In the process of the individual's becoming richer, society also becomes richer. Indeed the improvement of society is nothing more than the sum of the improvements of individuals. In a dynamic and improving society, therefore, the increase in riches of the individual is not thought of as a redistribution of wealth (one individual gaining at the expense of others) but rather as a creation of wealth (the gains of one individual representing net additions to the total and being taken from no man). [51]

Thus the Protestant ethic leads not only to individual success but to national prosperity as well.

The stewardship of wealth, so fundamental to the Protestant ethic, also plays an important role in Boulding's reassertion of the traditional values:

> Another doctrine which Protestantism shares with other forms of Christianity has combined with the "lost gospel" to contribute to the success of capitalist institutions: the doctrine of stewardship, of charity in the narrowest sense of the word. Those whose virtue, energy or plain good fortune have brought them material success are expected to regard their riches as in some sense a trust, to be used for the benefit of the less fortunate. Over the long pull, this aspect of Christian culture has proved of great importance in modifying the inequalities of capitalism. [52]

Boulding sums up his contribution by once again asserting his faith in the "lost gospel" of Protestantism, and by urging its relevance to modern economic conditions:

---

[51] Boulding, "Religious Foundations of Economic Progress," p. 36.

[52] Ibid., pp. 36-37.

Looking at a perspective of three or four hundred years, the Protestant economic gospel has been a fantastic success. It has created a society in which there is a smaller amount of serious poverty than any other society has ever known. It has fostered a tenfold increase in the population of the Atlantic world and has mastered a mighty new continent. [53] . . . If the Protestant church can rediscover and reinterpret its historic message and mission, it might prove the catalytic agent that would bring a new society into being. [54]

James C. Penney. If enthusiasm for the Protestant ethic has waned among some contemporary theoreticians and businessmen, there are others who still praise and exemplify in their own lives the qualities of the moral athlete. Both the life and the thought of J. C. Penney reflect these values. Born the son of a fundamentalist Baptist minister, Penney was schooled in the traditions of the Calvinist creed. He himself tells the story how at eight years of age, his father called him one evening to announce: "Jim, your mother and I have talked it over, and have decided that you are now old enough to buy your own clothes."[55] This was just the beginning of the young boy's training in thrift, industry, and frugality.[56] At the age of twenty-one he was forced by poor health to leave his Missouri home for a more salubrious climate, and later he summarized the religious influence during his early years at home:

As long as I was at home I went to church with great regularity and was much interested in Sunday school. Between these influences and my parents'

---

[53] Boulding, "Our Lost Economic Gospel, " p. 971.

[54] Ibid. , p. 972.

[55] Norman Beasley, Main Street Merchant (New York: McGraw-Hill Book Co. , Inc. , 1948), p. 4.

[56] James C. Penney, Fifty Years with the Golden Rule: A Spiritual Autobiography (New York: Harper and Brothers, 1950), p. 12.

courageous and high-principled example, I was setting out from home rich in spiritual capital. [57]

In business for himself a few years later, he set a pace
of extraordinary industry and frugality. His store opened
at seven each morning, with the concession of an eight-
o'clock opening on Sundays. His thriftiness and frugality
reflected his earlier home training. "I had been trained,"
he observes in his autobiography, "on my father's farm not
to waste a seed potato or an ear of corn or a squash seed.
Why should I waste string in the Kemmerer store, or nails,
or even a piece of wrapping paper?" [58] There was no doubt
in the young Penney's mind that his occupation was in harmony with his spiritual welfare. "Those were the days,"
he remarks, "when it was widely accepted that a man could
not create a fortune and, at the same time, be a Christian.
I wanted very much to disprove the idea, and to do both. I
believed it was possible." [59] Penney often asserted his
company was founded on religious principle:

> Our formula, rooted in a creative everyday
> practice of the golden rule by each individual in the
> organization, was the firm tradition of Christian liv-
> ing: "Respect yourself; respect others; work hard
> and continuously at some worth while thing" was our
> motto. Growth was the proof of its practicality. [60]

Penney's frugality was not one of necessity. It was a
religious principle which remained with him through the
years. In 1911, when he was already the head of a twenty-
two store chain grossing over a million dollars a year, he
described his company headquarters:

> The office was a room, about thirty by thirty-
> five, with a cement floor, one flat-top desk (loaned
> me by a friend), and one old-fashioned standing desk,
> which shrewd merchants of an earlier time had

---

[57] Ibid. , p. 34.

[58] Ibid. , p. 57.

[59] Ibid. , p. 68.

[60] Ibid. , p. 74.

devised on the principle that a bookkeeper who has to stand up to do his work will not be very likely to fall asleep and waste time.

I slit the envelopes of my mail, using the blank sides for scratch paper. We didn't have a typewriter, but did all work in longhand. When a pencil was needed, one of us went out and bought it for a penny. We bought ink in a bottle at a time, as we did penholders, with penpoints by the nickel's worth, as we absolutely had to have them.[61]

This is a truly remarkable account of frugality, but its motivation was not entirely economic. It was also religious. "It seems to me," Penney affirmed, "a mistake to draw an arbitrary line between the sacred and the secular, and that the measure of man's whole duty is the same for business, and for service to God."[62]

In his frequent talks on the relationship of business and religion, he reflects his conviction with respect to the importance of other qualities characteristic of the Protestant ethic:

As a seed must be buried in the cold, damp earth before its blossoms can emerge into the sunlight, so success must be preceded by sacrifice. Self-denial is a basic requirement for accomplishment, whatever the field of endeavor. Diligence in business results in advancement. Unselfishness invites good will, which, in turn, opens opportunities for material progress.[63]

My experience has been that employees respond to fairness and liberality.[64]

I take the prerogative of mature experience and urge younger men as they come along to study with great earnestness the relation between Christ's two

---

[61] Ibid., p. 102.

[62] Ibid., p. 171.

[63] Ibid., p. 177.

[64] Loc. cit.

commandments, to love God, and to love your neighbor as yourselves. [65]

Working these two great laws into the balance of
everyday life there is assurance of a life of spiritual
satisfaction and, I firmly believe, one of material
prosperity and peace of mind. [66]

If these are the values Penney found so successful in
his own life, he is equally sure that this same gospel of the
economic virtues will bring success to others:

Any young man or woman of ordinary intelli-
gence, who is morally sound, open and above board
in human dealings, not afraid of work, prepared to
play the game fairly and squarely and keep everlast-
ingly at it, can succeed in spite of handicaps and
obstacles. [67]

Is there any necessary conflict between ethical and
religious values on the one hand and the exigencies of the
business world on the other? Not as Penney sees it:

Nor do I believe, with many, that in facing the
so-called cold world of business it is necessary to
throw into discard the fundamental principles of honesty, fair dealing, and sobriety in order to succeed. [68]

Penney summed up his thought on the relationship between being a good Christian and being a good businessman
in the following revealing passage:

It seems to me that anyone inclined to question
whether one can be a business success and a good
Christian at one and the same time need look for re-
assurances no further than to the words spoken by
the Lord to Joshua, when he bade him lead the children of Israel across the river Jordan into the land
which was to be their home: "This book. . . shall not

---

[65] Ibid., pp. 180-81.

[66] Ibid., p. 181.

[67] Ibid., p. 197.

[68] Ibid., p. 200.

depart out of thy mouth; but thou shalt meditate therein day and night, that thou mayest observe to do according to all that is written therein: for then thou shalt make thy way prosperous, and then thou shalt have good success. "[69]

Penney, like Rockefeller, attributed his business success to the providence of God. The way to wealth he discovered in the Bible, and his final years have been devoted to spreading this gospel of wealth. [70] If the present age is somewhat drifting away from its traditional beliefs, James C. Penney has presented himself as a living testimonial to the agelessness of the Protestant ethic.

SUMMARY OF THE CHAPTER

This chapter has attempted to trace the influence of one factor in the formation of American business morals: the Protestant ethic. It began by exploring the theoretical basis for the link between the virtues of the Protestant ethic and the thinking of the early religious reformers. Then through three critical stages of American history the Protestant ethic was found influential, in both a theoretical and a practical way. Protestant theoreticians and businessmen were found to be asserting the values of the Protestant ethic both by word and by deed. Though there has been no effort to rank the importance of this influence on the development of American business standards, it is believed that the evidence of the chapter leads to the conclusion that the Protestant ethic has in fact been operative in the formation of these values, and that a better understanding of contemporary business standards will result from an appreciation of the influence of this Protestant ethic.

---

[69] Ibid., p. 244.

[70] Beatrice Plumb, J.C. Penney: Merchant Prince (Minneapolis: T.S. Denison and Co., Inc., 1963), p. 152.

Chapter 2

THE SOURCES OF AMERICAN BUSINESS ETHICS: THE JEWISH INFLUENCE

INTRODUCTION

THE IMPORTANCE OF THE JEWISH CONTRIBUTION

While the Protestant ethic has played a vital role in the formation of American business morals, it does not represent the only religious influence on the ethical conduct of businessmen. Among the other religious influences, the Jewish faith has likewise conditioned such conduct to a degree which at first may not be recognized. For although the Jewish people have remained a minority group in the United States, their cultural traditions and values have been such as to have naturally led these people to an excellence which could not for long remain unnoticed and unrecognized among the American people. And with this recognition of personal excellence, the religious and cultural values of the Jewish faith have been given a more-than-proportional role in the formation of American mores. As Woodrow Wilson has expressed it:

If we could but have the eyes to see the subtle elements of thought which constitute the gross substance of our present habit, both as regards the sphere of private life and as regards the action of the state, we should easily discover how very much besides religion we owe to the Jew. [1]

It is the task of the present chapter to investigate several of the values of the Jewish faith and to relate these values to the business environment.

---

[1]Cecil Roth, The Jewish Contribution to Civilization (New York: Harper and Brothers, 1940), p. 21.

WERNER SOMBART

The investigation of Jewish religious values is not an easy one. It has been made complex by several particular circumstances. The first of these is the work of the eminent economic historian, Werner Sombart. In 1911 he published his Die Juden und das Wirtschafsleben, which was subsequently translated into English under the title of The Jews and Modern Capitalism.[2] In this volume, Sombart argued that the spirit of Judaism and the spirit of capitalism complement one another in a remarkable way. As he saw it, the Jewish men of business were the primary molders of the capitalist system; and, consequently, capitalism could be looked upon as a child of the Jewish faith.

In many of the religious values taught in the Old Testament, Sombart saw the characteristics which made for capitalist system. The arithmetic concept of sin; the close relationship between religion and business; the exact and precise legal system which guided transactions of every nature; the virtues of prudence, foresight, moderation, and industry—all these fused together to form a religious spirit much akin and at home with the economic spirit and economic system which arose out of the ruins of the medieval artisan economy. Further, Sombart argued that the Jews were in an eminently suitable position to spread their ideas throughout European and colonial territories. As the Jews were persecuted and discriminated against in one country after another, they moved their enterprise, and with them their spirit, to other lands. Thus as the Jews were expelled and found shelter in one country after another, the trade capitals of Europe shifted from Spain to Holland, from Antwerp to Amsterdam, from Augsburg to Frankfort and Hamburg.[3] And as "Israel moved like the sun across Europe," the spirit of capitalism likewise moved; and this movement was due in good part to the spread of Jewish ideals and trade connections.[4]

---

[2]Werner Sombart, The Jews and Modern Capitalism (Glencoe, Ill.: The Free Press, 1951), 402. pp.

[3]Joseph Jacobs, Jewish Contributions to Civilization (Philadelphia: The Jewish Publication Society of America, 1919), p. 248.

[4]Howard Morley Sachar, The Course of Modern Jewish History (New York: Dell Publishing Co., 1963), p. 39.

Scholars today generally regard Sombart's theory as an oversimplification, not without a number of misconceptions and exaggerations. The Jews, of course, did play a significant role in the development of the contemporary economic system of the West. No doubt this system owes a great debt to the Jewish merchants and financiers who migrated across Europe. But the part these men played was not only that of molders. They were also the putty of the envolving social changes. If it is true that the Jews helped shape the destiny of capitalism, it is equally true that capitalism helped shape the destiny of the Jews. Certainly the racial and religious prejudices manifested against the Jews have played an important role in both the cohesion of the Jewish community and in their dispersion throughout many important commercial centers of the world. But these factors are in the last analysis to no small degree sociological and political in nature as well as religious.

With respect to his understanding and interpretation of the Old Testament, Sombart also manifests certain misconceptions. It is erroneous to infer from the frequent Biblical references to business matters to suppose that the Jewish faith was less oriented to good works and to the moral life than has been Christianity. If there are detailed prescriptions in the Old Testament concerning economic life, there are even more prescriptions and guides for the care of the poor, the obligation to love one's neighbor, and above all, the service of the temple. When the Hebrew faith is viewed as a whole, one is impressed with the profundity of its doctrine and its theocentric view of the world, a view which demands of the individual a whole response, a commitment which embraces every segment of his life. Judaism is far more than an economic gospel, and Sombart's misrepresentation is due in some degree to the failure to grasp this Gestalt approach to its content.

DIVERSITY OF JEWISH VALUES

There is another important reason why an investigation of Jewish religious contributions to American business morals is difficult: there exists today no single set of universally accepted Jewish values. Rather there are several sets of these values, and to some degree they contradict one another. The contemporary Jewish community, particularly the American Jewish community, is divided; and in some respects this division is fundamental. It concerns the basic scope of Judaism, whether Judaism is to be viewed as a whole way of life, embracing a cultural and social as well as religious activity, or whether its primary nature is solely religious.[5] Such a difference of opinion is one which undoubtedly has many beneficial results. As discussion among Jewish intellectuals progresses, a deeper and more penetrating appreciation of the Jewish heritage results.[6] But at the same time it presents difficulties to the student who looks for a simple and unequivocal expression of Jewish religious values as the basis for an investigation of the contemporary moral climate of American business.

This present investigation proceeds with these limitations in mind. There is need to make a sincere effort to avoid the type of simplicity which led such an eminent scholar as Sombart to receive the almost universal criticism of modern-day scholars. It is also important to recognize the complexity of modern Jewish thought. Accordingly, in the following section an attempt is made to analyze what are believed to be several significant and operating contributions of the Hebrew faith to the moral climate of American business. At the same time, an assertion that such values represent a set of values or a complete view of the Jewish position is deliberately avoided.

TWO JEWISH RELIGIOUS VALUES

THE LOVE OF LIFE

One value which runs almost universally throughout Judaism, and which stands in marked contrast to Christian values, is what might be called the Jewish "appreciation of

---

[5] Horace Meyer Kallen, Judaism at Bay (New York: Block Publishing Company, 1932), p. 182.

[6] Sachar, op. cit., p. 532.

life." Albert Einstein has considered this to be one of the most outstanding values of Jewish thought. As he put it:

> To the Jew, life is the highest worth, that upon which all other values depend. It is the affirmation that all creatures are holy, and the most acceptable form of service and adoration of God can be found in the basic respect for all creatures, concern for the now.[7]

This value, of course, reaches its apex in the Jewish respect for the human person.

This attachment to life has a profound influence upon the Jew's attitude toward reality about him. For while the Christian is somewhat withdrawn from the material world, the Jew is fundamentally and religiously involved with it. The Christian attitude has been described as "other-worldly." He is convinced that this life is not as important as the next, that, indeed, life on earth is a preparation for the more important life which is to come. While many Jewish expressions of faith profess belief in a future life, there remains a fundamental difference in orientation to the present world. The Hebrew faith teaches the present life has a great, even ultimate value in itself—this in contrast to Luther's belief, for instance, that the present world is basically unimportant, or to Calvin's view that worldly affairs serve only as a useful distraction, or at best, as a sign that all goes well in respect to the perplexing problem of predestination. The Jewish appreciation of life is far more direct and indeed far more profound than this. There is a basic and absolute value in living, not just a relative or utilitarian value. As Joseph Hertz, the late Chief Rabbi of the British Commonwealth, eloquently expressed it: "Israel's Faith is a religion of life, not death, a religion that declares man's humanity to man as the most acceptable form of adoration of God."[8]

---

[7]Albert Einstein, "Of the Jewish Religion," in Lee Schwartz (ed.), A Golden Treasury of Jewish Literature (New York: Rinehart, 1937), p. 756.

[8]Joseph Hertz, The Pentateuch and the Haftorahs (London: Soncino Press, 1956), p. 397.

This value is so deeply rooted in Jewish religious teaching that it is almost taken for granted, and its significance is likely to be overlooked by the Christian who approaches the Bible with a somewhat different value system. Nevertheless, the Old Testament itself can be looked upon as a primary source of this attitude. A psalm believed to be written by David around 1,000 B.C. crystallizes this belief:

> Turn, O Lord, save my life;
>> deliver me for the sake of the steadfast love.
> For in death there is no remembrance of thee;
>> in Sheol, who can give thee praise?[9]

This same attachment to life is reflected in the historical Books of the Old Testament as, for instance, in the account of a sickness which came upon King Hezekiah:

> In those days Hezekiah became sick and was at the point of death. And Isaiah the prophet, the son of Amoz, came to him, and said to him, "Thus says the Lord, 'Set your house in order; for you shall die, you shall not recover.'" Then Hezekiah turned his face to the wall, and prayed to the Lord, saying "Remember now, O Lord, I beseech thee, how I have walked before thee in faithfulness and with a whole heart, and have done what is good in thy sight." And Hezekiah wept bitterly. And before Isaiah had gone out of the middle court, the word of the Lord came to him: "Turn back and say to Hezekiah the prince of my people, 'Thus says the Lord, the God of David your father: I have heard your prayer, I have seen your tears; behold, I will heal you; on the third day you shall go up to the house of the Lord. And I will add fifteen years to your life.'"[10]

In both of these cases there is reflected a value quite distinct from the Christian attitude toward life. For the Christian, this life is a pilgrimage, a time of trial. Its actual length is not so important as how the individual leads

---

[9]Psalm 6, vv. 4 and 5. All quotations of the Bible are taken from the Standard Revised Version (New York: Thomas Nelson and Sons, 1952).

[10]2 Kings 20, vv. 1-6.

his life.   The Jewish faith is, of course, concerned with a
virtuous life.   But it also regards life itself as one of God's
major blessings to be highly valued in itself. [11]

This same attachment to life has prevailed through
post-Biblical Jewish history and has been an important
and distinguishing trait between Judaism and Christianity.
Howard Morley Sachar, one of the most competent of contemporary Jewish historians, has testified to the importance of this value to the very uniqueness of the Jewish
contribution to the West:

> The uniqueness of Judaism was its rejection of
> the indifference to life which characterized the pagan
> world; and its corollary rejection of emphasis on life
> in a world-to-come — an emphasis which, with a few
> notable exceptions . . . seemed to characterize Chris-
> tian doctrine until very recent times.   Reverence for
> life on earth was basic; it was concretized in count-
> less Jewish regulations, injunctions, and blessings
> covering the most prosaic as well as the most sacred
> deeds of man's daily life; it was symbolized in the
> cryptic phrase with which Jews toast each other,
> L'Chaim — To Life.   The concept has been abused
> and pulpiteered, but its vulgarization has not drained
> it of its validity: the passion for life counted as a
> more effective instrument than economic and political
> factors in enabling the Jews to survive as a people
> down to modern times. [12]

Clearly, then, attachment to life is a fundamental
element in the value system of the Jewish culture.   And it
is a value which is rooted in the specifically religious
traditions of this culture.   A subsequent section will explore its position in the contemporary mores of the businessman.

---

[11]The distinction here is a subtle one, but nonetheless real. It is
more a question of emphasis than theological dispute.   The Christian's
view of future life does not belittle the value of life on this earth.   For
the Christian, too, life itself is one of God's major blessings.   But
since the fullness of human existence is to be achieved in the hereafter,
there is in Christian thinking perhaps less of an absoluteness or finali-
ty about concern for the present life than is found in Jewish thought.

[12]Sachar, op. cit. , p. 399.

SOCIAL CONSCIOUSNESS

Another important value of the Jewish faith, and one not unrelated to attachment to life, is what might be called "social consciousness." Like a corresponding virtue of Christianity, Zedakah, as expressed in Hebrew literature, is concerned with the individual's obligation toward the poor, the weak and the underprivileged. But this Jewish awareness of social responsibilities goes beyond the reality of almsgiving and beneficence. For the religious Jew recognizes as most fundamental his relationship to a group. As one famous Jewish scholar has said:

> It is our destiny to live for what is more than ourselves. Our very existence is an unparalleled symbol of such aspiration. Being what we are, namely Jews, we mean more to mankind than by any particular service we render. [13]

Indeed, so fundamental is this awareness, that the real dignity of the individual is seen precisely as a participant in the group. As Alfred J. Kutzik expresses it:

> In spite of the grating sound it makes in the liberal ear, it must be stated that "the dignity of the individual" is not a Jewish value. This is so in spite of the widely recorded and readily observable fact that the individual is highly valued by the Jews. For the Jewish valuation of the individual derives from and is inseparable from his worth as a member of the community. Far from lessening the worth of the individual, this approach has resulted in an unusually high regard for the individual human being, giving rise to such famous Talmudic sayings as: "He who has saved one life, it is as if he has saved the world," and the principle and practices of pekiach nefesh whereby all the laws of Judaism may be abrogated to save a single life. [14]

---

[13] Abraham Joshua Heschell, "The Meaning of Jewish Existence," from Harold U. Ribalow (ed.), Mid-Century (New York: The Beechhurst Press, 1955), p. 92.

[14] Alfred Kutzik, Social Work and Jewish Values (Washington D.C.: Public Affairs Press, 1959), pp. 13, 24.

This value of social consciousness, like the value of attachment to life, finds its origin in the pages of the Old Testament. For the relationship of the individual Jew to God takes on its profoundest meaning by reason of the fact that he is the member of a people especially chosen by God. It is with the Jewish people as a whole, not with the individual Jew, that God has established his Covenant and made his promises. In the most solemn of these Covenants, made to Moses on Mount Sinai, the Book of Exodus records the intimate connection between the people of Israel and God:

> Thus you shall say to the house of Jacob and tell the people of Israel: You have seen what I did to the Egyptians, and how I bore you on eagles' wings and brought you to myself. Now therefore if you will obey my voice and keep my covenant, you shall be my own possession among all peoples; for all the earth is mine and you shall be to me a kingdom of priests and a holy nation. These are the words which you shall speak to the children of Israel. [15]

Sociological and political factors may have augmented this Jewish sense of belongingness, but at its roots this attitude is fundamentally a religious one.

Indeed, the historian Baron has advanced the theory that the fundamental Jewish value is precisely the preservation of the Jewish people. [16] Although this position has been challenged by conservative religious leaders, [17] it has attracted support by other Jewish scholars, most notably Simon Dubnow (1860-1941). [18] The controversy is far from settled, but its very discussion points to the importance of social consciousness in the hierarchy of Jewish values.

---

[15] Exodus, c. 19, vv. 3-6.

[16] Salo W. Baron, The Social and Political History of the Jews (New York: Columbia University Press, 1936), I, 39-43.

[17] Hertz, op. cit., p. 502.

[18] E. g., Simon Dubnow, Nationalism and History, Essays on Old and New Judaism (Koppel Pinson, (ed.); Philadelphia: The Jewish Publication Society of America, 1958).

From its very beginnings, then, the Jewish faith has placed a particular importance in the individual's membership in the group and in particular the specific group which was chosen by God as His People. But through the centuries this value has taken on new dimensions. Kutzik describes this evolutionary process in the following terms:

> Roughly in order of historical and psychological development, they [i.e., the stages of evolution of this value] appear to be: the worth of the Jewish people; the worth of all people; the worth of all communities, groups and persons; and the worth of life, and the value of all that preserves and enchances it. [19]

This evolution toward universalism can be found quite early in Jewish history. Indeed, it has been described as a significant element in the growing awareness of the Jewish people of their mission as the chosen people of God. [20] Thus the Biblical story of Ruth, which may be as old as four centuries before Christ, [21] is an account of a gentile woman who became the wife of the Jew Boaz and thus became an ancestress of King David himself. The lesson is unmistakable: particularism which excludes the gentile world is unwarranted. This same spirit of universalism is found in the writings of Hillel (ca. 110 B.C. — ca. 10 A.D.): all people are equal and fraternal love is to be extended to one's fellowmen of any race. [22] And the same universalism is again reflected in the answer to a question posed in the Talmud: "Why was man created a solitary human being, why were there not created several Adams and several Eves at one time?" The answer is given: "So that it might not be said that some races are better than others." [23] And

---

[19] Kutzik, op. cit., p. 24.

[20] Milton R. Konvitz, "Judaism and the Democratic Ideal," in Louis Finkelstein (ed.), The Jews: Their History, Culture and Religion (New York: Harper and Bros., 1960), II, 1431.

[21] Joseph Frank, Literature from the Bible (Boston: Little, Brown and Company, 1963), p. 143.

[22] Kutzik, op. cit., p. 22.

[23] Konvitz, op. cit., p. 1436.

to Ben Azzai, a great Jewish teacher of the second century, A.D., the most inclusive Jewish law was contained in the verse, "In the day that God created man, in the likeness of God he made him, male and female he created them" (Gen. 5:1-2). This verse, Ben Azzai taught, expressed unequivocally the equality and dignity of all human beings, irrespective of nationality, sex, color, creed, or genealogical origin. [24]

Thus the value of social consciousness grew from a concern for the Jewish group as a nation to concern for society as a whole. In fact, one of the most noteworthy Jewish philosophers of the early twentieth century, Hermann Cohen, saw this evolving social consciousness as one of the most powerful influences in Judaism, providing the basis for a whole code of Jewish ethics.

> In fact, for Cohen Judaism was a kind of "Religion of Reason," a religion which encouraged its adherents not to attain communion with God or to find personal salvation — pagan ideas according to Cohen — but rather to strive for the ideal society, the society of moral perfection. [25]

To strive for the ideal society, the society of moral perfection, is, then, an important value in the Jewish heritage. The personal experience of social injustice and discrimination has, indeed, given the Jew a deeper appreciation of the significance of this value, and has undoubtedly motivated him to participate in activities aimed at furthering social justice. But at its roots the value is a religious one, one which is an integral part of the relationship established between the God of Israel and his chosen people. This value, like the attachment to life, has become a part of the American creed, and has played a significant role in the development of American business mores, a role which will be explored more at length in subsequent sections of this study.

---

[24] Louis Finkelstein, "The Jewish Religion: Its Beliefs and Practices," in Finkelstein, op. cit., II, 1750.

[25] Sachar, op. cit., p. 411.

AMERICAN JEWISH VALUES

The discussion above investigated two Jewish values as they were rooted in the biblical sources of Jewish tradition and as they have been modified through the evolution of Hebrew theological development. The present section attempts to study the modifications which these qualities have received through their contact with the American environment. No cultural group in the United States can claim to be unaffected by the American milieu. Rather the values of every culture which has been implanted on American soil have been affected and modified both by the influence of other immigrant cultures and by the peculiarly unique characteristics of the American people. If this is true of immigrant cultures in general, it is especially true of the Jewish cultural traditions. For the American Jewish community itself is a mixture of several variant cultural traditions as different waves of immigrants provided leadership to the group and gave it their own spirit. German Jews, for instance, took an early leadership, provided a liberal orientation, and became champions of a modernized, "deorientalized," and "Anglicized" Jewish community. Later, Russian immigrants viewed with suspicion such leadership and urged loyalty to traditional orthodoxy both in doctrine and in practice.

In another respect, too, Jewish values have been modified and influenced by their exposure to the American culture. Jewish scholars have frequently noted that in spite of the presence of some prejudice and discrimination, the Jew has enjoyed in America a degree of freedom and acceptance unparalleled in Jewish history. [26] This has led to a certain degree of assimilation of the Jewish community into the general pattern of American life. Some Jewish values have been so influenced by this Americanization of the Jewish populace that certain scholars view it with alarm and warn against the present tendency of many Jews to sever their ties with their religious traditions and practices. [27] Others of the same outlook call for a reaffirmation

---

[26]Sachar, op. cit., p. 342.

[27]Kutzik, op. cit., p. 36.

of a totally Jewish Weltanschauung.[28]   Such discussion
within the Jewish community points to the need to study the
two values described above in the light of their uniquely
American expressions.

POSITIVE ACCEPTANCE OF WEALTH

The traditional Jewish value of attachment to life has
been influenced both by Eastern-European ideals and by
materialistic standards of success.   Students of American
Jewish culture observe that in the United States this value
has taken the form of a nonasceticism, a love or appreciation of life's pleasures.[29]   Thus in the American Jewish
hierarchy of values there is wide acceptance of wealth as
a value in itself, a worthy object of man's striving and endeavor.   This value stands somewhat in contrast to the
Christian view of wealth, which, at least in its dogmatically
pure form, regard possessions as something of a   threat
to the Christian virtues of poverty and detachment and the
like.   The Christian doctrine of stewardship attempts to
reconcile the possession of riches with the spiritual dangers such possession involves, and to a degree this doctrine
does provide the Christian with a defense against these
dangers.   But Christianity and wealth — God and Mammon —
make at best an uneasy union.   American Reform Judaism,
on the other hand, presents a direct acceptance of wealth
as a value in itself.   Not that the concept of stewardship is
wholly absent from the Jewish tradition, or that wealth has
become the ultimate value of Jewish life.   Far from it.
The prophetic literature of the Old Testament abounds with
exhortations to charity and the use of wealth for the benefit
of the unfortunate.   Nevertheless, this striking appreciation of life's pleasures and the wealth which makes them
possible stands in contrast to traditional Christian values.

It must be admitted that this American orientation
toward the love of life's pleasures has not been received by
all Jewish thinkers with unmixed emotions.   There is a

---

[28]Mordecai Menshem Kaplan, Judaism as a Civilization (New
York: T. Yoseloff, 1957), 601 pp.

[29]Lawrence H. Fuchs, The Political Behavior of American Jews
(Glencoe, Ill.: The Free Press, 1956), p. 178.

problem here. The distinction between a direct acceptance of wealth and a materialistic spirit which lauds the accumulation of wealth for self-satisfaction is a fine one. But it is a distinction which is absolutely essential if Judaism is to preserve its theocentric and social orientation. An unreserved commitment to the accumulation of wealth is simply not a religious quality – neither Jewish nor Christian nor any other. The problem is that attachment to wealth may become an attachment to American standards of success which have no particular relationship to any religious values. And if such nonreligious goals take precedence over genuinely religious ideals, then it may be that a religious crisis is in the making. Indeed the crisis may also be a moral one. It is not simply that ethical standards are changing; they may also be vanishing, and unmitigated self-advancement may be replacing traditional ethical values as criteria for conduct.

Some Jewish sociologists fear that the situation in the American Jewish community is getting dangerously close to this.[30] They are somewhat disturbed by what they believe to be the growing ascendancy of wealth as a primary symbol of success at the expense of the traditional Jewish value of Torah, learning. Learning and education, first in respect to the Law and then with respect to other disciplines, have traditionally been viewed in the Jewish culture as superior to the possession of wealth. Some scholars are fearful that wealth is becoming the most widely accepted standard of success, and they warn that if such appreciation of life's pleasures is not rooted in the grateful acceptance of creatures as gifts of God, this quality loses its religious significance.[31] In this respect, Jewish values may be in danger of the same erosion which faces Christian faiths as well. Rather than a specifically Jewish concern, this problem in all probability is basic to all deeply rooted religious groups in America.

---

[30]Salo W. Baron, "The Challenge of Material Civilization," in Leo W. Schwartz (ed.), Great Ages and Ideals of the Jewish People (New York: Random House, 1956), c. 16, pp. 391-419.

[31]Salo W. Baron, "The Dynamics of Emancipation," in Schwartz, Great Ages . . . , c. 13, p. 331.

RECOGNITION OF SOCIAL RESPONSIBILITIES

It has been asserted that the American Jewish community exhibits in an unprecedented way the Zedakah which
has characterized the long and varied history of the Jewish
people. [32]   To a small degree this may be accountable to
the remarkable economic success of American Jews. Their
devotion to education and the economic freedom which
has been theirs have led them naturally to an economic
status which exceeds both that of the average American and
also that of Jews in other nations. [33]   But more important,
perhaps, is the fact that the Reform Jews of the United
States have never been overoccupied in matters of doctrine
and liturgy.   The major expression of their faith has been
through concern for the broad issues of our society relating
to social justice. [34]   Thus they have been exceptionally
active in those areas which involve community responsibilities.   In one direction this quest for social justice has
found expression in the extraordinarily impressive record
of Jewish philanthropy in America. In 1962, for example,
five and one-half million Jews contributed over $165,000,000
to Jewish charities which used these funds to support a
wide variety of both Jewish and non-Jewish welfare programs. [35]   This generosity of the American Jewish community to works of philanthropy is one of the most striking
characteristics of this minority group.   Not only does such
philanthropy stand out in the quantity of funds raised, but
even more important, it exhibits an almost scientific dedication to the efficient use of these funds to further an
extraordinarily broad program of aid.   Jewish welfare
philanthropy touches almost every aspect of human welfare
and has become to no small degree a model of efficiency
for other religious and charitable groups.

---

[32] Kutzik, op. cit. , p. 35.

[33] Simon Kuznets, "Economic Structure and Life of the Jews, " in
Finkelstein, op. cit. , II, 1641-42.   See also Nathan Glazer, "Social
Characteristics of American Jews, " in Finkelstein, op. cit. , II, 1721.

[34] Sachar, op. cit. , p. 522.

[35] Morris Kertzer, "Jewish Affairs," in Collier's Year Book,
1962 (New York: Crowell-Collier Publishing Co. , 1963), p. 339.

In another direction, the Jewish religious value of social consciousness or social responsibility has had a profound influence. The Jewish community has exhibited an unusually active interest in the broad social problems of the American culture. A sense of social responsibility and a conviction of the efficacy of social action have led Jewish leaders into the areas of civil liberties, antidiscrimination activities, concern for international social problems, and also into political life. Indeed, this interest in social responsibility finds its expression, in part at least, in the relatively high percentage of Jews who enter one of the professions: law, medicine, education, politics, and the like. There are undoubtedly many complex motivations which lead to the choice of such professions for a lifework, but it seems hard to explain this predilection without recognizing a basic orientation to this value of social responsibility.

JEWISH VALUES IN BUSINESS PRACTICE

INTRODUCTION

The previous sections of this chapter have attempted to describe several Jewish values as they are rooted in the authentic sources of Jewish theology and as they have been interpreted by the American Jewish community. The present section is directed to appraising the role these values play in the business community.

There is to some degree a conceptual difficulty in demonstrating a causal influence between a value system and concrete events of the historical order. While facts of history may be uncovered and scientifically investigated, it is much more difficult to ascertain the motives and ideological influences behind such facts. This section will attempt to show such an influence in two steps: first, it will be shown that the values described in the previous section are in fact found in the business community. Secondly, several case studies will be presented of prominent Jewish businessmen who exemplify these values.

It may be objected that while these values are found in the American business environment, such values are not exclusively Jewish in origin. This point is readily admitted.

For it is not the object of the present argument to prove that Jewish traditions were the only, or even the most important, influences in the development of the standards of American businessmen. Such is obviously not the case. Indeed, the present value system of Americans is so intricately and inextricably intertwined with contributions from many cultures that the attempt to ascribe some values to a single cultural influence would be naive and contrary to one of the major propositions of this study: that the present standards and values of American business are the product of a distinctively American culture mix. What is aimed for here is to demonstrate that Jewish traditions have had some influence in the formation of these values. Accordingly it will be sufficient to show that these values fundamental to the Jewish religious heritage are in fact found in American business.

JEWISH VALUES IN THE AMERICAN BUSINESS COMMUNITY

Positive Acceptance of Wealth. The United States has been described as a country which has traditionally espoused the Protestant ethic as its conventional wisdom. [36] And yet there is a striking presence, some would say prevalence, [37] of values which are fundamentally opposed to the conventional wisdom. Positive acceptance of material prosperity both as a national and personal goal is an instance of this countercurrent in the conventional wisdom. Certainly the alleviation of poverty is a noble aspiration of the Protestant ethic as well as other religious and humanitarian creeds. But the acceptance of wealth as such, characteristic of American business, is something quite different. It has become a standard of success for both the individual and the nation. This success criterion cannot be adequately explained in terms of self-interest alone. Self-interest undoubtedly plays an important role in most ideologies. But

---

[36]William Hollingsworth Whyte, The Organization Man (New York: Simon & Shuster, 1956), p. 4.

[37]C. Wright Mills, The Power Elite (New York: Oxford University Press, 1956), pp. 9-10. See also David Morris Potter, People of Plenty (Chicago: University of Chicago Press, 1954), pp. 190-208.

the point has been convincingly made that the confidence, emotion, and fervor with which the standard of wealth is professed and accepted in the United States gives evidence of a raison d'etre which goes beyond self-interest, a raison d'etre which is rooted in moral and intellectual convictions concerning the value of "the good life."[38]

A large segment of the business community accepts wealth, not with the reserved stewardship rationale of the Protestant ethic, but rather in a positive and direct manner. Moreover, this acceptance is more than an expression of the material ambitions of the individual. It is proposed as an American value. This value is a frequent theme, indeed, one of the dominant themes in literature praising and defending the American business system. A classical example of this value is found in a pamphlet of the Advertising Council, Inc., entitled "The Miracle of America":

> Today the American way of life provides the highest standard of living ever enjoyed by any people in the world.
>
> This is no mere boast. It is a statement of thrilling fact—that men can raise their level of living by greater productivity if they are free to do it.
>
> Electricity, running water, central heating, one house or apartment per family are quite general in America. To the Russian or Chinese worker, whose whole family is often crowded into one room, with no private kitchen or bath and no central heating, our homes would represent dreams of luxury.
>
> With only one fifteenth of the world's population and about the same proportion of the world's area and natural resources, the United States—has more than half the world's telephone, telegraph and radio networks—more than three quarters of the world's automobiles—almost half the world's radios—and consumes more than half the world's copper and rubber, two thirds of the silk, and a quarter of the coal and nearly two thirds of the crude oil. [39]

---

[38] Francis X. Sutton, et al., The American Business Creed (Cambridge, Mass.: Harvard University Press, 1956), pp. 12, 13.

[39] Ibid., pp. 19-20.

And an Allis-Chalmers advertisement expresses the same appreciation of material wealth: "Millions of machines turned out canned goods, cars, textiles, radios—better and better each year. There is no stopping Science and Industry now . . . no limit to good things to come."[40]

The legitimacy of the quest for wealth as an American value is expressed on the personal level as well as on the macroscopic level:

> Search history as we may, and we can find but two motives which have stimulated man to economic activity beyond the most meager requirements of subsistence. These two motives are (1) the desire for personal advancement and (2) fear . . . . The desire for self-aggrandizement may be evidenced by the purchase of the finest yacht afloat. It may also be expressed in the much less obtrusive personal satisfaction which comes from doing well for one's family and appearing well before one's neighbors. Fear is fear . . . .
>
> . . . Personal advancement is whatever raises the individual in his own estimation. Such increased self-esteem may come with clothes and jewelry. It may come from the ability to contribute largely to charities. It need not be and usually is not, unworthy. The personal desires most Americans strive to satisfy are decent and honorable.[41]

And Burlington Mills, in an advertisement in the New York Times, identifies the marks of wealth with the "good life":

> A refrigerator. You can live without it.
> A yellow convertible car. You can live without it.
> A television set. A Chippendale chair. . . .You can live without any or all of these.
> But who in America wants to?
> In America, these things represent LIFE rather than mere subsistence. In America the things we don't need for mere existence are more important

---

[40] Ibid., p. 48.

[41] Ibid., p. 101.

than the bare necessities, so abundant in this land.
Take ribbon—gaily colored ribbon. . . .[42]

The Recognition of Social Responsibility. The same students of
the contemporary business creed who find a strong emphasis in the appreciation of life's pleasures also point to a
definite current social responsibility in American business.
Indeed, some scholars identify the proponents of social
responsibility as representing one of the major "strands"
of the creed:

> In fact, we must distinguish between two strands
> of thinking in the American business creed, which
> differ substantially on certain points in their treat-
> ment of the American System as well as throughout
> the creed in general. We shall call these two strands
> of thought the "classical" and "managerial" versions
> of the creed. The classical strand centers around
> the model of a decentralized, private, competitive
> capitalism, in which the forces of supply and de-
> mand, operating through the price mechanism, reg-
> ulate the economy in detail and in aggregate. The
> managerial strand differs chiefly in the emphasis it
> places on the role of professional managers in the
> large business firm who consciously direct economic
> forces for the common good. [43]

A number of executives have given public allegiance
to the social responsibilities embodied in the managerial
strand of the business creed. There is among such men a
recognition that corporate decisions have an impact on the
whole of American society and the values which this society
professes. A businessman cannot ignore this dimension of
his decisions. As W. T. Gosset, Vice-President and General Counsel of the Ford Motor Company, has observed,
it is:

> necessary for modern management to consider
> how the facts and realities in a corporation's affairs
> will square with the public philosophy, with the values

---

[42]Ibid., p. 255.

[43]Ibid., pp. 33, 34.

of the total national community and its sense of where it is headed. [44]

To be sure, the businessman may not have gone out to seek these social responsibilities, but nonetheless he has found corporate decisions are related to the public philosophy in many ways. As Gilbert W. Fitzhugh, President of Metropolitan Life Insurance Company, explains it:

Does the corporation seek these responsibilities, or are they thrust upon it? Actually, it's neither one. They are there. They are inescapable. They are part of the warp and woof of the society in which we live.

Is the corporation comfortable with these responsibilities? This is irrelevant. We have got them whether they are comfortable or not. We must do our best to measure up to them if we are to do our job for our stockholders or policyholders as well as for our country. After all it is really the same thing. [45]

A number of executives relate social responsibilities to the higher goals of society, as do the executives quoted above. And when such is the case, the doctrine of social responsibility goes beyond economic self-interest, even long-run profit maximization. It represents a commitment of the corporation to the same values of a democratic society which individuals make. J. Irwin Miller, Chairman of the Board of The Cummins Engine Company, has effectively expressed this responsibility in respect to one fundamental value of democracy—freedom:

A loss of freedom or an impairment of rights or property for any man diminishes my freedom and my rights. This is the lesson of the free society about which we are concerned.

For its own freedom, for the maximum pursuit of its own property interests, the corporation, like

---

[44] Richard Eells and Clarence Walton, Conceptual Foundations of Business (Homewood, Ill.: Richard D. Irwin, Inc., 1961), p. 458.

[45] In "Company Responsibility—Too Much or Not Enough?" A panel discussion, The Conference Board Record, I(4) (April, 1964), 10.

the individual, must make a free response to the
society of its time.   Its response must be aimed at
the good and the improvement of that society.   It is,
therefore, in our desire for a free society that we
begin to find the reason for the social responsibility
of a corporation. [46]

The point that needs to be made here is that this value
of social responsibility is found in the business creed.   It
is probably true that it does not represent the dominant
strand in the creed, but it is nonetheless a strand which is
very much alive and very much the subject of controversy.
It is a call for the businessman to look beyond self-interest
and to determine the social consequences of his business
policies.   As one executive has described the dimensions of
this new look:

> Social responsibility is a many-faceted thing.
> Our first responsibility is to make a good product and
> provide as good a service as we can at an economical
> price so that the public will buy from us.
>
> We have a second responsibility to be a good
> employer to the people that work for us. And we have
> a third responsibility to the community in which the
> corporation lives, the town, the state, the country,
> or the trading area. [47]

Not infrequently the proponents of social responsibility
see its need in relation to the economic prosperity of the
businessman: it is precisely because the businessman has
been so successful that he has the responsibility to regard
his wealth and power with consideration of the welfare of
the community at large.   In some respects, this is a kind
of stewardship concept, but it is directed to the justification
of the possession of wealth and power vis-a-vis society
rather than from a personal ascetical viewpoint.   Thus O.
Kahn argues that the businessman, as one of the primary
possessors of wealth in the United States, needs to consider
this wealth as a public trust, and consequently, needs to
consider social parameters of business decisions:

---

[46] In "Company Responsibility – Too Much or Not Enough?" p. 9.

[47] Gilbert W. Fitzhugh in Ibid., p. 10.

The undisturbed possession of the material rewards now given to success, because success presupposes service, can be perpetuated only if its beneficiaries exercise moderation, self-restraint, and consideration for others in the use of their opportunities, and if their ability is exerted, not merely for their own advantage, but also for the public good and the wealth of the fellow men. Democracy rightly insists that a part of every man's ability belongs to the community. [48]

Thus the two values discussed in this chapter are not considered as unrelated by many members of the business community. On the contrary, they are intimately connected, the former depending upon the latter. The material prosperity as enjoyed by the businessman is his precisely because the general public recognizes the service nature of business activity. If this public trust is not to be violated, the businessman needs to look to the common welfare which is affected by his economic decisions. According to this theory social responsibility and economic prosperity go hand in hand. [49]

Thus it can be seen that the business community does to no small degree accept the same values which have characterized the American Jewish community. A positive acceptance of wealth as a personal and national goal, and the acceptance of social responsibility as a duty are fundamental and distinctive values of the Jewish religion. They are also strands of what has been called the American Business Creed. It is not contended that the acceptance of these values has been precisely due to the fact that they are elements of the Jewish faith. The causal relationship between these ideals of the Jewish faith and those of American business cannot be measured; but just as it is improbable that these business values can be adequately explained by religious ideals alone, it seems equally improbable that the sincere religious convictions of a prominent group of

[48] Sutton, et al., op. cit., p. 249.

[49] For a development of this theory, see Adolph A. Berle, Jr., The Twentieth Century Capitalist Revolution (New York: Harcourt Brace and Co., 1954), Ch. 2, "Corporate Power and Modern Capitalism," pp. 25-60.

American businessmen have had no influence whatsoever on the formation of business ideals. The truth lies somewhere between these two extremes, and though we may never be able adequately to gauge it, Americans have drawn on the traditions of the Hebrew faith in the formation of their national scale of values.

TWO CASE STUDIES: JEWISH BUSINESSMEN IN PRACTICE

A CASE STUDY: AARON LOPEZ [50]

The story of the Jews in colonial Rhode Island is very much the story of Aaron Lopez. Born in Portugal in the eighteenth century, Lopez was raised in a family which had to practice its Jewish faith in secrecy. Lopez landed in Newport, Rhode Island, in 1752 and very soon became one of the leading merchants and shippers in the English colonies. So successful was he that it is reported the entire city of Newport felt the impact of his business activity. He owned, in whole or in part, some thirty transatlantic ships and over one hundred coastwise vessels which constantly plied between harbors with cargoes of lumber, fish, horses, whale oil, molasses, and rum. He had representatives in numerous ports of call, in both the New World and the Old. In a very short time he had become one of the most successful and prosperous of the colonial merchant traders.

Lopez was deeply religious and followed orthodox Judaism with exemplary fidelity. No ship ever left his dock on a Sabbath Day. He exhibited in his actions both of the Jewish values described in the previous sections. He entertained royally in his home, and the magnificence of his table attracted Newport's highest society. He also manifested the deep sense of social consciousness characteristic of his beliefs. He devoted considerable time to community works and was noted for his efforts to establish friendly relations between Christians and the large Jewish community

---

[50] The details of this life are drawn from Henry Simonhoff, Jewish Notables in America – 1776-1865 (New York: Greenberg, Publisher, 1956), and Anita Libman Lebeson, Pilgrim People (New York: Harper and Bros. , 1950), 624 pp.

of Newport. Through his charity and attention he was able
to establish some forty Jewish families in the community
at Newport. He was one of the founders of the Newport
Public Library, and the local synagogue was built at his
expense.

The American Revolution brought ruin to Newport, and
Lopez lost the substantial part of his vast holdings. In 1872
Lopez was killed by a bolting horse as he returned to Newport to rebuild his trade empire. Charles H. Russell, a
contemporary of Lopez, wrote of his death:

> Thus was removed in the meridian of life one
> of the most eminent and useful merchants that New-
> port ever had. His death, at the period it took place,
> may be considered one of the greatest misfortunes
> that ever befell the town. Cut off as he was, pre-
> paring to renew his various enterprises, there can be
> no doubt from his extensive business relations, that
> had he lived, he would have speedily retrieved his
> losses and greatly contributed to revive the business
> and trade of the place. He was a man of eminent
> probity and benevolence. His bounties were widely
> diffused. They were not confined to creed or sect,
> and the people of Newport for more than half a cen-
> tury continued to venerate his memory.[51]

A CASE STUDY: BERNARD M. BARUCH

As the life of Aaron Lopez embodied the achievements
of the colonial American Jewish community, so the life of
Bernard M. Baruch was representative of the achievements
of the contemporary Jewish community. Born in 1870 in
Camden, South Carolina, Baruch was raised in a decidedly
American and Southern family environment. Nevertheless,
both his parents were strongly committed to the Jewish
faith and communicated this commitment to their children.
Bernard's father, Dr. Simon Baruch, had proposed and
supported a Hebrew Sabbath School in Camden, and his
children were among its few faithful pupils. In 1880, at
the time of his resignation as President of the local Hebrew
Benevolent Society, Dr. Baruch expressed his views on

---

[51]Quoted in Charles P. Daly, The Settlement of Jews in North
America (New York: P. Cowen Co. , 1893), p. 86.

religious education. In a letter to the Society's membership he wrote:

> As parents and Jews it is your most solemn
> duty to educate your children not only mentally but
> morally also. . . . Thus only will you enable them to
> become useful citizens who by their upright life and
> moral excellence will afford examples . . . to other
> sects and shed lustre on Judaism. . . . [For the
> doctrines of Judaism] as expressed in the Book of
> Leviticus and especially in the Ten Commandments
> form the basis of the moral laws of all civilization. [52]

These ideals of faith and ethics were communicated to the
young son of Dr. Baruch as a part of his heritage.

In modern times Bernard Baruch became somewhat a
person of controversy within the Jewish community, for he
never became vigorously active in exclusively Jewish religious activities or philanthropies. In addition, some of his
opinions caused misunderstanding among a vocal minority
of the Jewish community. The Orthodox took offense at his
external observances; the liberals found him excessively
conservative; and the Zionists berated him for his open
opposition to the founding of Israel. This lack of any clear
identification with any partisan segment of the Jewish community was coupled with a strong sense of patriotism.
Margaret Coit has illustrated this latter trait in a little
anecdote concerning a conversation between Baruch and a
prominent Rabbi:

> "Aren't you ever going to do anything for your
> people?" the Rabbi asked.
> "You're damned right I am," Baruch replied,
> "I'm going to do everything I can for my people.
> They're the American people." [53]

It is understandable that such strong positions have
given rise to misunderstandings.

But if a vocal minority has taken exception to this
attitude, many other Jews have recognized in Baruch an

---

[52]Margaret L. Coit, Mr. Baruch (Boston: Houghton, Mifflin Co.,
1947), p. 25. Words within the brackets have been added.

[53]Coit, op. cit., p. 671.

authentic expression of the Jewish faith. Baruch himself, in spite of criticism, throughout his life remained enrolled in the West End Synagogue, New York, and bitterly resented charges that he was lax in fulfilling his religious obligations. In this respect he seems to have followed the attitude of his father. While he reverenced and practiced the tradition of his faith, he saw this faith more as a way of life than as a body of orthodox dogma, and he practiced his faith more by a moral and upright life than by adherence to external ritual practices. And Jewish leaders have recognized his contribution to both his religion and his country by means of numerous Jewish awards.[54]

Baruch's life clearly exemplified the American Jewish values of attachment to life and recognition of social responsibilities. From a very early age he was a wealthy man and used his wealth quite freely to enjoy the finest goods of life. His years of public service stand as a monument to his sense of social concern. But it is particularly his early years, while he was still active in business affairs, which have relevance to the present study.

It was through the years at the turn of the twentieth century that Baruch acquired his wealth and became famous for his business acumen. As a young broker and speculator on the Stock Exchange he moved in a world in which regulation was minimal and free-wheeling was normal practice. Baruch was a part of this world, and his conduct cannot be judged by contemporary standards. And yet in many ways Baruch's business activities reflected the social responsibility which has been described as characteristic of American Jewish values. His sense of personal responsibility for his broker activities on the exchange eventually led him to withdraw from making transactions for others.[55] He regarded his position on the Exchange as a membership in a profession and was convinced that the Exchange could continue to thrive only if its members practiced the high ethical standards of the other professions.[56] Baruch himself became a member of the Governing Committee of

---

[54]Who's Who in America, 1964-5, Vol. 33 (Chicago: Marquis — Who's Who, Inc., 1964), p. 121.

[55]Coit, op. cit., p. 99.

[56]Loc. cit.

the Exchange and worked toward the discovery and punishment of delinquent members. He was proud of the degree of self-regulation and control exercised by the Exchange but likewise asserted such regulation did not go far enough. When in 1934 the Securities and Exchange Commission was established, he expressed the belief that there was need of this government control and defended the Commission by pointing to the fact that the Exchange had not provided enough protection for the small and nonprofessional investor.[57]

As Baruch grew older he began to turn his attention more fully to public affairs, and to a great extent his business career came to an end. But it would be a mistake to consider this manifestation of a deep social consciousness as a sudden and unprecedented conversion. Rather it represented a gradual and deepening awareness of the importance of directing his life to the service of society. And as Baruch passed from the business world to the world of statesmen and diplomats, it is not too much to assert that he was motivated by the same sense of responsibility with which he guided his business career and which found its source in his religious heritage.[58]

SUMMARY OF THE CHAPTER

This chapter has investigated in part the contribution of the Jewish faith to present-day business morals. Two fundamental values were chosen as illustrative of this contribution, and their relationship to the religious traditions of the Hebrew culture were established. Next these values were considered as they have been modified by various cultural influences in America, and their evolution into a positive acceptance of wealth and a commitment to social responsibility was described. Then these values were discussed as they are found in contemporary business mores. Finally two case studies were presented of American Jewish business leaders who exemplified these values in their business activities.

---

[57] Loc. cit.

[58] Bernard Baruch died in June of 1965.

Chapter 3

THE SOURCES OF AMERICAN BUSINESS ETHICS — CATHOLIC VALUES

INTRODUCTION

As has been previously noted, the Catholic influence in the formation of American values has not been as prominent as the Protestant influence. Several factors are accountable for this circumstance. Except for the experiment in the Maryland settlement, which was short-lived as a "Catholic" endeavor, there is little evidence of a strictly Catholic tradition predominant in the English colonies. [1] Undoubtedly, as has been the case with the Jewish tradition, there are strong reasons for this lack of influence upon the part of Catholics. The colonial leaders were, for the most part, Protestant in faith; and the religious struggles of English Civil War were too close in the past to remove all suspicion of the Catholic population. Catholic immigrants frequently found their place in the lower strata of American society and often were not given full political rights. Early discrimination and attacks on the Church led the Catholic population to develop what John Tracy Ellis has called an "increased separateness of Catholics from their non-Catholic neighbors."[2] Later waves of Catholic immigrants found themselves entering a society already molded by the values of Protestantism; and since the new arrivals were generally of the lower classes, like other immigrants to American shores, they found their places

---

[1] John Tracy Ellis, American Catholicism (Chicago: University of Chicago Press, 1956), pp. 22-27. Although the Catholic tradition was much more observable in the Spanish and French colonies, these latter settlements contributed less to the main cultural stream of the new nation.

[2] Ibid., p. 81.

among the unlettered and uninfluential working classes of the new continent. Catholics were slow to take their proportionate place among the intellectual, political, and business elite of the new world; and thus the influence of Catholic traditions has been less than that of the Protestant founders of the United States.

Nevertheless, it is profitable to examine several strands of Catholic thought which are presently rooted in American traditions and to trace their expression and development on the American scene. Catholics today represent a significant minority in America; and their religious traditions have, somewhat belatedly, entered into the cultural stream of American life.[3] Further, the Catholic Church, especially since the Papacy of Leo XIII (1878-1903), has made a positive and deliberate effort to interpret its dogma in the light of the great social and economic issues of the day. Catholics in America have been particularly responsive to this effort. The Annual Statements of American Hierarchy have frequently turned to social and economic issues.[4] A great body of literature has been published in the United States in connection with two great encyclicals on the social and economic order: Rerum Novarum (by Leo XIII, 1891) and Quadragesimo Anno (by Pius XI, 1931). To some degree, then, Catholic expressions of the Christian content have been in circulation since the turn of the century.

As in the study of Protestant and Jewish values, the Catholic values which are about to be explored are not Catholic in the sense that they are exclusively found within the Catholic community. Nor, indeed, is there any intention of asserting that these values find their origin exclusively in Catholic thought. Rather, these values are Catholic in the sense that Catholics have found them particularly apt expressions of their view of interpersonal and social relationships among men, and that Catholics find a deep religious and theological significance to these values.

---

[3] Adolph A. Berle, The American Economic Republic (New York: Harcourt, Brace and World, Inc., 1963), p. 192.

[4] For example, The Pastoral Letter (1919), Bishops' Statement (1933), The Church and Social Order (1940), The Christian in Action (1948), God's Law, Measure of Man's Conduct (1951), and Discrimination and the Christian Conscience (1958), to mention but a few.

That these values are shared by a majority of Americans of all faiths, does not diminish the fact that they present to Catholics a religious synthesis of man's relations with his fellowmen. Because Catholic theology has traditionally and consistently viewed social and economic problems through the focus of these values, they provide a suitable means of understanding the spirit of the Catholic approach to social and economic relations.

TWO VALUES IN CATHOLIC THOUGHT

Much of Catholic social theory can be derived from the basic concept of man which is part of Catholic tradition. Basically, man is regarded as possessing a twofold aspect to his nature: an individual aspect deriving from the reality of his person, and a social aspect deriving from his need to associate with other persons. Each of these aspects needs explanation.

THE DIGNITY OF THE INDIVIDUAL PERSON

An appreciation of the worth of the individual human being is a value common to the Western tradition of social thought. But within the perimeters of Catholic thought, this concept is central to the Catholic's synthesis of the relationships which should exist in the social sphere. This concept of personal dignity draws support from the disciplines of both philosophy and theology.

Catholics adhere to an Aristotelian concept of man: A being composed of body and soul, whose supreme dignity is derived from his spiritual nature. Reason and free will are the highest activities of human nature, and by reason of these activities man is unique among all the beings of the world. Because man has a spiritual aspect to his being, he possesses a dignity and value which is simply above the purely material order of reality. Thus the individual person cannot be regarded solely as a means, as this would imply a denial of the full reality of his being.[5]

To this dignity of the human person as expressed in Greek philosophy, Catholic theology adds another dimension

---

[5] Aristotle, Nicomachean Ethics, especially Bk. I, c. 13. Cf. W. D. Ross (translator) Ethica Nicomachea (London: Oxford University Press, 1931), 1102a - 1103b.

— the sacredness of the human person. If philosophy reveals man as the highest form of life on earth, theology reveals man as created in the image and likeness of God. "Then God said, 'Let us make man in Our image, after Our likeness. . . .' So God created man in His own image, in the image of God He created him."[6] Because of this fact of creation the individual takes on a new dignity and is the object of a new reverence which lies much deeper than a recognition of the biologically complex organism which is solely the result of natural forces.

This theological concept of the individual's sacredness is deepened by the theological doctrine of the redemption of mankind. Because of Christ's death, a new importance has been given to the human person, and it becomes an essential part of the Christian vocation for the Catholic to live in such a way as to give expression to this sacredness of his fellowmen. "A new Commandment I give to you, that you love one another; even as I have loved you, that you also love one another."[7] The Catholic, then, is to conceive of his vocation as fulfilled in his dealings with his fellowmen. Interrelationships among individuals are not just an appendage of his worship of God; they become an integral part of this worship. They are not mere signs of predestination; they are the means whereby the Christian, ultimately responsible for his own activities, works out his salvation by a positive and deliberate effort to live by the ideals which Christ taught.

THE SOCIAL NATURE OF MAN

Another value found in Catholic theology which to some degree guards against excessive individualism is the social nature of man. As man is seen by nature and by divine predilection to have a basic and inviolable dignity, so too he is seen by nature and divine design to be a social being. His needs and objectives cannot be satisfied by his isolated activity alone. Rather, by his physical and biological limitations, he is naturally ordered to join with his fellowmen in society to achieve his basic needs. Organized society is

---

[6]Genesis, I, vv. 26-27.

[7]John, XIV, v. 34.

not by its nature a hostile force opposing the ideal of individual personal dignity, but rather is the natural means of obtaining the circumstances in which personal dignity can be recognized and cultivated. Indeed, without a well-ordered social organization, human dignity for a vast number of individuals may be unattainable. The opportunities for the individual to develop his full potentiality is greatly conditioned by the character of the social institutions which influence his daily existence. Further, the individual Christian performs many of his activities in the framework of social organizations, and his vocation as Christian extends equally to those activities as well as to the activities which he performs in his own name alone. Hence Catholic values have historically been related not only to the individual but also to both formal and informal organizations.

Like the dignity of man, this sense of the social nature of man finds its expression in the Aristotelian tradition of Greek philosophy, and this leads the Catholic to see the harmony between the spheres of natural reason and revelation. Aristotle conceives of man as a social animal, for as he has expressed it: "He who is unable to live in society, or who has no need because he is sufficient for himself, must be either a beast or a god."[8] Thus both the family and the state are "natural" societies — societies whose existence is rooted in the very exigencies of human nature.

But this social nature of man goes deeper to a religious source. The Catholic believes that while Christ's message was a deeply personal one, He also founded a visible society, a Church, to guard His teachings and communicate them to succeeding generations through time. The Church is a formal society, a visible social institution which the Catholic recognizes as the instrument of Christ's activity in every generation. Thus the necessity of seeking one's salvation, not alone, but as a member of a society founded by Christ, is very central to Catholic teaching. The acceptance of the formal organization of the Church, with its hierarchy, dimensions, and channels of authority, is considered natural in the sense that God chose for the dispensation of His supernatural graces, a form which is so much in accord with the natural tendencies of man.

[8]Aristotle, Politics, I, 2. Cf. Richard McKeon, (editor). The Basic Works of Aristotle (New York: Random House, 1941), 1253a (p. 1130).

Activity that is distinctively social, then, is seen as part of the economy of salvation. God has established an order in which man must work for his salvation in society. Thus both philosophical and theological analyses points to the congruency of social participation in satisfying both the spiritual and material needs of man, and man's activities in society are a part of his general vocation to live as a Christian in the world.

This attitude contributes to an understanding of Catholic theology's traditional interest in the individual's role in society and of the Church's insistence that such a relationship is part of the dispensation of salvation. Teaching with regard to the family, education, the economic order, and political societies has always been considered by the Church as relevant to the religious life of its members. The medieval concept of Christendom, the whole world united into a harmonious community (while national allegiances remained), though never fully realized, was perhaps the closest approximation of this ideal.

This same social awareness permeates more recent Catholic thought. Order has been the word which has expressed the fulfillment of Catholic ideals of social relationships.[9] It would be a mistake to identify too quickly this order with rigidity or social immobility, though in certain periods its expression did take this form. In feudal society, order could be interpreted as maintaining the political structure of the age; in the guild period, order could mean providing each citizen with the means of livelihood sufficient to maintain his social status. But in other times it has also meant giving to the working class a greater share of the economic product or forming new international organizations to resolve the obstacles to world peace.

These theological values of the dignity of the individual and the social nature of man are not, of course, exclusively the belief of Catholics. Indeed, they are part of the Christian, and to some degree, part of the Judeo-Christian heritage. Nevertheless, Catholicism has seen in these truths a foundation for a social stance toward the world

---

[9]For example, Pius XI's Encyclical, Quadragesimo Anno has been translated into English with the title: On the Reconstruction of the Social Order.

which might be characterized as truly Catholic. And this stance is the key to the Catholic's approach to the problems of business conduct in the modern world.

EXPRESSION OF THESE VALUES IN CATHOLIC SOCIAL DOCTRINE

This ideal of order finds its expression in concrete economic life through the concept of justice. Indeed, it was through relationships of justice that the Catholic was to transfer to action his abstract ideals of the dignity of the individual and his sense of community. Justice became the source or guide for preserving the proper respect towards others while at the same time seeking one's own legitimate self-interest.

This Christian concept of justice grew from the Greek and Roman concepts as expressed by the ancient philosophers. [10] Plato conceived of justice as a bond which held the state together. It was the condition which made it possible for men with competing and conflicting goals to live together in harmony. He defines justice as "giving every man his due," but it is in his development of "what is due" that Plato makes this thought clear:

For "what is due" to the individual [according to Plato] is that he should be treated for what he is, in the light of his capacity and training, while "what is due" from him is the honest performance of those tasks which the place accorded him requires. [11]

Plato stresses the concept of obligation contained in justice. By reason of obedience to civil authority, social harmony is maintained. This obedience is rendered by the individual not through the fear of sanction if this duty is not observed, but rather through an interior conviction of

---

[10] For an excellent summary of the Greek and Roman traditions of justice cf. Richard Eells and Clarence Walton, Conceptual Foundations of Business (Homewood, Ill. Richard D. Irwin, Inc.), pp. 318-324.

[11] George H. Sabine, A History of Political Theory (New York: Holt, 1950), pp. 54-5. See also: Plato, The Republic, Book IV, "Definition of the Four Virtues."

order — the need of the individual to subordinate his activities to the good of the state.

Roman tradition stressed another dimension of justice: the rights of the individual and the duty of the state to protect these rights. Justice under this concept views the individual both as the subject and as the object of personal rights. He has certain rights which are his own; other individuals, too, have rights. Civil authority has the function of insuring that all citizens will honor the rights of their fellow countrymen. Hence, justice hinges on the concept of equality before the law, and the state becomes the protector of the individual. [12]

St. Thomas fundamentally accepts both the Greek and Roman concept of justice and affirms further that the source of justice lies above the state itself and rests in the fundamental integrity of the human person. Thus civil authority, while central to a just society, is not the fundamental source of rights. The state protects basic human rights, but does not bestow them. Rather they flow immediately from the religious fact that God created man with a dignity and a sacredness which no other creature may rightly ignore.

On the practical level, the Catholic sees justice as guiding human activity on two levels: the interpersonal level and the social level. On the interpersonal level, the relationship of one individual with others, justice provides the individual with the disposition to give to other individuals what is their due. Scholastic theologians of the middle ages studied this aspect of justice and developed a rather sophisticated body of principles to help the Christian concretely obtain this goal. On another level, justice is concerned with the individual's duties to society, or to the furtherance of the common good, and with society's duties to the individual. It is by the application of both of these concepts of justice to the social problems of the age that their influence can best be understood. The basic issues of social problems can be resolved by understanding the application of both social and individual justice. Several examples will illustrate the operational reality of these concepts of justice.

---

[12] Eells and Walton, op. cit., p. 321.

PRIVATE PROPERTY

The institution of private property provides a good illustration of the application of both individual and social justice, for its justification springs from both the individual and the social aspect of man. Following Aristotle, St. Thomas Aquinas, an outstanding authority among medieval theologians, finds the desire to possess private property "natural" to man. Man alone of all creatures has a concept of futurity, and with it the drive to provide for his needs not only in the present, but also in the future. Private property is the only institution which makes it possible for the individual to face the exigencies of his future needs with the assurance that they will be adequately provided for. By the accumulation of private possessions, the individual is able to convert his diligence and industry into provision for his future needs. Thus the desire for private property springs from the basic desire of self-preservation; and where the right to such possessions is denied the individual, he will lack the security and the independence which flows from such security to pursue his existential goals in a manner consonant with his human dignity. [13]

Aquinas lists other arguments which are supportive of the individual's need for private property. Men are naturally led to familial life as the normal pattern of living. In such a society, there is need for the head of the family to provide not only for his own needs but also for those dependent upon him for support. Without the right to acquire private property, the head of the household cannot provide for his dependents in matters such as the education of his children, the support of his family in the case of his own incapacity, the provision for himself after the time of his retirement. Private property provides a suitable means to meet such exigencies in a manner in accord with human dignity. Further, private property represents one of the most suitable means for the individual man to achieve a sense of creative development and accomplishment. For the economic aspect of a man is so much an integral part of his full being that the full development of the human personality would be lacking without the opportunity of

---

[13] St. Thomas Aquinas, Summa Theologica. Secunda Secundae, Quest. 66, art. 2. (London: Burns and Oates, 1929), Vol. 10, p. 224.

acquiring dominion over some of the goods of the economic order.

At the same time Aquinas and the other theologians of his time were equally emphatic that private property also was demanded for social motives. Private ownership serves a social function inasmuch as all the goods of the earth are for the benefit of all men. Private ownership provides an efficient manner to ensure that such goods will be used in an efficient way. Privately owned goods will be used and developed more effectively than will goods that are held in common possession, and thus will contribute more to society than if they were not owned by a single individual. Individuals naturally take better care of those things which are their own. By the institution of private property, therefore, the material goods are better ordered to the satisfaction of human wants. [14]

Other considerations support this social function of private property. Where there is a clear understanding of what is the possession of each member of society many disputes are avoided, and social harmony is promoted. In a productive society, a natural problem arises concerning the division of goods produced. Without private property, such controversies can be resolved only by political authority. Such a method of settlement of the division of economic goods is likely to result in some abridgment of the individual's political freedom. Again, private property provides the basis of an exchange economy and the benefits of trade which naturally result from it. If all productive property is commonly held, the ability to trade, with its concomitant benefits to both parties, is restricted to that recompense which an individual receives in exchange for his own personal labor. And this would be decidedly less advantageous than if a greater scope is given to the mechanism of trade.

Catholic social thought has developed from this early analysis of St. Thomas and the scholastics. Private property is vigorously defended in Catholic social thought. At the same time, both the individual and the social aspects of property are also considered. [15] In its individual aspect,

[14] Loc. cit.

[15] Pius XI, Quadragesimo Anno, para. #46. Reprinted in Seven Great Encyclicals (Glen Rock, N. J.: The Paulist Press, 1963), p. 137.

property is seen as natural to the individual, contributing substantially to his development and his dignity as a human being.   At the same time, the control or right of private property is not considered as absolute.   Property is to be used in such a way as to contribute to the social good. [16]   In this sense, the concept of stewardship, common to both Protestant and Jewish theologies, is expressed with a different emphasis in Catholic social writing.   Property is not held simply as a gift of God, by which the use or abuse of this gift is answerable to God; rather, property must be used in such a way that it is beneficial to society as a whole; the individual property owner is answerable to society as well as to God.   Further, society has the right, even the duty, to lay down rules in the use of property to ensure that it will be used in a manner beneficial to all.   Thus the traditional Catholic formula states that while ownership should be private, the use of goods for the owner's benefit must also be consonant with the common good. [17]   For example, if wealth is superfluous in the sense that it is not needed to satisfy the private necessities of the individual, it should not be allowed to remain idle.   Rather it should be put to some use that will be socially beneficial.   Pius XI has spelled out in detail how this might be done.   He suggested that one of the principal forms of munificence today is the investment of funds in the production of goods which are truly useful to the economic community.[18]   Not only does this add to the store of goods which are available for consumption, but such a use provides jobs and economic activity, both of which contribute to a prosperous economy.

THE JUST PRICE

Another application of this twofold concept of justice to the economic sphere can be seen in the development of the theory of the just price in Catholic thought.   Basically, the

---

[16] John XXIII, Mater et Magistra, para. #43.   Reprinted in Ibid. , pp. 227-8.

[17] Pius XI, Quadragesimo Anno, para. 45.   Reprinted in Ibid. , p. 137.

[18] Pius XI, Quadragesimo Anno, para. #50-51, reprinted in Ibid. , p. 139.

problem arises from a consideration of the demands of commutative justice, justice guiding the relationship of individuals among themselves. Obviously one of the most notable ways the rights of an individual can be abused is by taking unfair advantage of him in economic exchange. Buying and selling to some degree involves a conflict of interests. The task of the Catholic theologian has been to work out a norm whereby an exchange could be completed which was mutually advantageous to each party, one in which the rights of each party were protected. However, the problem of the just price also has social overtones. For at stake in the pricing mechanism is not just the welfare of the individuals concerned in the single exchange, but the welfare of the community as well.

Scholastic discussion of the just price has gone through an evolutionary development as theologians have come to understand more completely the nature of economic exchange and as the market institution itself has changed from a feudalistic to a capitalistic character. The Franciscan John Duns Scotus (d. 1308) was one of the first to embody the theological ideal of human dignity into a practical measure of a just price. Scotus reasoned that just as it was obvious that a merchant could earn his livelihood by his commerce, it was equally obvious that a just price could be measured against his success in attaining this end. If the merchant gained excessively so that he was able to live above his station in life, then it was evident that his prices were too high. On the other hand, if the merchant was forced to sell his goods at such a price that he could not adequately maintain his family in its proper state, then he was the victim of an unjust price. Thus for Scotus the key to a fair price was that it should be such that the difference between the merchant's cost of production and his selling price provided him with an acceptable standard of living. Consequently, Scotus' analysis centered around the cost of production:

> All the expenses have to be taken into account, whether incurred in the purchase, transportation, or preservation of the merchandise. Then there should be added a just reward which is merited by the industry, labor, and risk of the merchant. [19]

[19] John Duns Scotus, De Justitia et Jure, IV, Dist. 15, quest. 2, art. 2.

Scotus' norm was a great contribution to scholastic analysis of the marketplace. It embodied the traditions of both philosophy and theology with respect to business transactions, and at the same time presented an eminently practical norm—one which became an immediate guide to the tradesman.

But as the economic life of the Middle Ages grew more complex and as the scholastics became more cognizant of the market institutions which were arising in the latter part of the Middle Ages, they saw a competitive market price as best reflecting the fair price of a commodity. By the middle of the sixteenth century, the communis aestimatio was widely accepted as the norm of a just price. Basically, if a merchant sold his goods for the current price in a free market, then he could be sure that his price was fair. For where many buyers and sellers met, there arose a common price based on many judgments as to the value of a particular good at a given time and place. This was the communis aestimatio, the just price for a given market. As Luis Molina, a Jesuit theologian of the Sixteenth Century, expressed it:

> And so the just price of objects depends in no small way on the common estimation of men in the particular region concerned—when, without fraud, monopoly, or other deceit, an object for sale is customarily sold for a certain price. [20]

Thus by the end of the sixteenth century scholastics had affirmed a pricing theory based on a capitalistic market structure. The market itself was recognized as the best norm of a fair price. But it was a healthy market which was to be used as the foundation of this norm. If a monopolistic market, or a market otherwise imbalanced existed, a simple market price might not represent a truly just price. Then the merchant acquired a new obligation, one related to social justice, to contribute as far as he was able to the establishment and maintenance of equitable market structures. If citizens were abused by artificially high prices, it was the duty of the businessman to take what

---

[20] Luis Molina, S. J. , De Justitia et Jure (Bosquet: Collegium Allobrogorum, 1733), Vol. II, Tr. 2, d. 348, p. 230.

steps he could to bring about such market conditions that the welfare of the consumer could be protected.

The important point to note here is that the scholastics saw this essentially economic activity as related to the concept of justice and consequently to the study of theology. Schumpeter has observed that the scholastics developed an incipient price theory which was later explicitized into the price mechanism of classical economics.[21]   But fundamentally their concern was morality, and their greatest contribution was to express the need for the application of both commutative and social justice to the pricing function of economic life.

APPLICATION OF THESE VALUES TO THE AMERICAN SCENE

Both the concept of private property and that of the just price have received considerable attention from American Catholic authors as they attempt to relate Catholic social principles to economic and social conditions of the United States.   And the effort of these spokesmen to interpret Catholic principles in the light of a distinctly American culture gives further insight into the nature of Catholic social thought.

PRIVATE PROPERTY: A MEAN BETWEEN LIBERALISM AND SOCIALISM

Applications of the traditional Catholic concept of property have gone through several phases in American Catholic social thought.   During the decade immediately preceding the turn of the twentieth century and several decades following it, emphasis was put on the social aspect of property.   Under the inspiration of the famous encyclical of Leo XIII, Rerum Novarum, Catholic authors stressed the obligations of proprietors to use their property in such a way as to benefit the common good.   In particular, the concept of property as providing for the material necessities of all citizens became the motif of a social message

---

[21] Joseph A. Schumpeter, History of Economic Analysis. New York: Oxford University Press, 1954), pp. 97-8.

which condemned the abuses of unbridled free enterprise.
To be sure, consideration was given to the distribution of
the economic product of the great enterprises which were
bringing the United States to a new appreciation of the
fruits of industrialization.   But emphasis was put also on
the duty to use capital with a special regard for its social
effects.   And this line of thinking led Catholic authorities to
a criticism of a purely liberalistic concept of capitalism.

This purely liberalistic theory of capitalism as outlined by Adam Smith and championed by such men as David
Ricardo, Thomas Malthus, and John Stuart Mill, posited a
number of rigid economic laws which invariably brought
about that a man who sought his own economic self-interest
would, by some unseen force, also make a maximum contribution to the social group.   In the famous words of Adam
Smith, the individual "intends only his own gain and he is in
this as in many other cases led by an invisible hand to promote an end which was no part his intention. "[22]   And since
the social good took care of itself, the individual could
concentrate on his own personal economic gain.   Thus he
best served society by seeking his own economic advancement without any concern for the social effects of his decisions.   The market mechanism harnessed self-interest in
such a way that not only did it provide a solution to the
allocation and distribution problems of economic society, it
also provided a solution which was so natural that it could
not be avoided without violence to the "natural laws" of the
economic science.

Catholic thought was opposed to this liberalistic interpretation of capitalism for several reasons.   First of all,
liberalism was based on a concept of individualism which
in practice denied the social nature of man.   By concen-
trating solely on the individual aspect of man, it professed
that no attention need be paid to his social aspect.   This
would take care of itself, a sort of necessary by-product of
self-interest which has been allowed full expression.

In another, and in some respects, in a more fundamental way, liberal capitalism was opposed to Catholicism.
In practice, liberalism adopted the concept of economic
success as the basic criterion for human success.   While

---

[22]Adam Smith, Wealth of Nations (New York: Modern Library,
Random House), p. 423.

Catholic theory recognized the importance of the economic welfare to the well-being of men, nevertheless it insisted that the human person has goals and ends which go beyond the perimeters of economic analysis and that spiritual values must always take priority over economic values. The production of economic goods, important as it is, should not be organized in such a way as to maximize the economic output at the cost of more fundamental values. Inasmuch as liberalistic capitalism implied an economic materialism, it opposed the basic values of Catholicism. It is highly dubious that such a system ever existed in reality on American shores. But such an interpretation of capitalism was proposed as an ideological model of the industrial society of nineteenth century American business.

But Catholic writers of the last century and the first part of the present century spoke against the ideological system as failing to recognize the degradation of human dignity which often accompanied the use of private property. Wealth was for man, not man for wealth. And the production of wealth which resulted in such widespread inequalities and injustices was forcefully condemned. As Leo XIII expressed in his encyclical of 1891, "there can be no question whatever, that some remedy must be found, and quickly found, for the misery and wretchedness which press so heavily at this moment on the large majority of the very poor."[23] As Catholics in America repeated this warning, they found themselves in opposition to the popular philosophy of the times, and this undoubtedly contributed to the fact that their voices were often ignored.

The Church's attack on liberalism was leveled against both elements of its philosophy. The social aspect of property was emphasized: the duties the proprietor has toward other members of his society. Basically, these duties resolved into the obligation to use his wealth in such a way that its use resulted in a furthering of the common good. It was not enough for the wealthy man simply to give to the poor out of his largess, though this was, of course, encouraged. The actual property from which this largess flowed was likewise to be used in a way beneficial to the general public. The right of the state to regulate, control, and direct the use of wealth for the common good while

[23] Leo XIII, Rerum Novarum, op. cit., para. #2. Reported in Seven Great Encyclicals, op. cit., p. 2.

preserving its private nature was firmly defended against the extremes of liberalism which regarded all governmental interference as unjustifiable.

On the other hand, the Church defended her twofold concept of property against another philosophy of the nineteenth century: excessive collectivism. For while property was to be used for the benefit of all, its private character was to be preserved as that form of ownership which was most in accord with the exigencies of human nature. Papal documents abound with condemnation of doctrinaire socialism and communism as incompatible with the Christian concept of the nature of man.

The Church's position in America was not simply voiced in a negative way — through the opposition to liberalism and collectivism. The positive presentation of the twofold nature of property was carefully charted through an application of the theory of subsidiarity. As expressed by Pius XI:

> It is a fundamental principle of social philosophy, fixed and unchangeable, that one should not withdraw from individuals and commit to the community what they can accomplish by their own enterprise and industry. So, too, it is an injustice and at the same time a grave evil and disturbance of right order to transfer to the larger and higher collectivity functions which can be performed and provided for by lesser and subordinate bodies. [24]

This principle becomes a key guide in understanding the relationship between the individual and the social nature of property. Property is first of all private, and that by reason of its relationship to the nature of man. But property must be used in a means that is beneficial to society as a whole, and thus the larger political organization of men has the right and the authority to determine the conditions of private ownership so that these social objectives can be attained. Government regulation of private property, under this scheme of things, is not then an evil in itself, not even a necessary evil. It is intrinsic to the very nature of property.

----

[24]Pius XI, Quadragesimo Anno, op. cit., para. #79. Reprinted in Ibid., p. 147.

Thus while the Church encouraged social legislation as a necessary safeguard against the evils of liberalism, it likewise warned against an excessive intervention of the state into private affairs which would lead to an equally dangerous form of collectivism.

THE JUST WAGE

The principle of the just price found special application in the American economy with respect to the discussion of the just wage. The equitable reward for labor was to be determined by the basic principles of justice and was the object of both individual and social justice.

Wages are the reward for productive effort. As such, they are capable of pricing just as any other commodity on the economic market. If the theory of the <u>communis aestimatio</u> is applied to determine the fair wage for any given skill, then the going wage of labor becomes the just wage according to this theory. Since the going wage is determined by the forces of both supply and demand, this wage is subject to change and variation, according to circumstances, skills, time, and place. Further, the rate may well be determined, as are other prices in a competitive economy, by the bargaining of both the sellers and the buyers of labor. The basic obligation of individual justice, then, is for the employer to pay a wage that is in general line with the going rate for the various skills in his locality.

However, to this basic application of individual justice, other considerations must be added. In a real sense, the worker, while he is a supplier of a commodity in the market, is far more than that. As an individual human being, he represents an end of the economy as well as one of its ingredients. The purpose of the economy is to provide for the material needs of the citizens of a given society. In modern economic life, labor is the chief and often the only avenue of the vast majority of citizens to the fruits of the economy. Thus for the economy to function well, the rewards for labor must be such that they provide a suitable living standard for the working class. This reasoning has led to the concept of the living wage.

In addition to the basic obligations of individual justice, then, the employer has an obligation in social justice, an obligation to work toward the condition where the individual wage of the worker will at least be equal to the amount needed to live in a manner in accord with his human dignity. If at any particular time, for instance, in a serious depression, the going rate of labor is not equal to this minimum for decent subsistence for the worker and his family, then there is a further obligation of the employer: to work for social reform that will bring the wage rate up to minimum standards of living. It should be noted that this theory does not propose that the employer is obligated to pay more than the market rate for labor at any time. To assert such an obligation would be to put an impossible burden on the employer, to put him at a competitive disadvantage which would place his economic survival in jeopardy. But he should recognize the social evil which is present, through no fault of his own, and do what he can to bring about the conditions in which the worker can receive a fair share of the economic produce of the economy. [25] Thus, as Pius XI expressed in his Encyclical: The Reconstruction of the Social Order:

> Every effort must therefore be made that fathers of families receive a wage large enough to meet ordinary family needs adequately. But if this cannot always be done under existing circumstances, social justice demands that changes be introduced as soon as possible whereby such a wage will be assured to every adult working man. [26]

Application of this theory of the just wage was slow to take hold of American Catholics, particularly due to a fear that socialist tenets dominated the early American Labor Movement. [27] It was not until James Cardinal Gibbons defended the cause of the Knights of Labor before Leo XIII (1887) that Catholics turned in earnest to the application of the just wage to the American economy. Particularly

---

[25] John F. Cronin, Social Principles and Economic Life, (Milwaukee: The Bruce Publishing Co., 1959), p. 209.

[26] Pius XI, Quadragesimo Anno, para. #71. Reprinted in Seven Great Encyclicals, op. cit., p. 145.

[27] For a further development of this thought, Cf. Rita Joseph and Robert L. Reynolds, "Catholics and U.S. Labor," Jubilee, Vol. 2 No. 5 (Sept. 1954), pp. 37-49.

through the efforts of the articulate and prolific writer Msgr. John A. Ryan were the ethical applications of the social encyclicals made the basis of a Catholic social philosophy in the United States. Ryan became the spokesman of Catholic social thought through the first forty years of the present century and is in no small part responsible for the development of a well-defined body of principles applicable to the American Labor Movement. Today Catholic labor schools and Catholic labor — management institutes continue the traditions of this early movement and adapt it to the changing conditions of the American economy.

SUMMARY OF THE CHAPTER

This chapter has investigated the influence of Catholic thought on the American economy by explaining the fundamentally Catholic approach to social problems. It was seen that Catholic social philosophy stresses the application of two concepts of man — his individual aspect and his social aspect — as necessary to avoid the extremes of excessive collectivism and excessive individualism. These two approaches to the human person were seen as the foundation for a social theory of property and pricing. The application of these concepts to the American economy were illustrated through a discussion of both private property and the just wage in the United States.

Chapter 4

REVIEW OF RELATED LITERATURE AND DESCRIPTION OF THE QUESTIONNAIRE

INTRODUCTION

RELATION OF PART II TO PART I

The purpose of this part of the study is to investigate contemporary business ethics. Part I of the study provided a background for understanding the present milieu of American business morals. It investigated several historical influences which appear as conditioning the present situation. Because of the impossibility of adequately discussing the wide variety of historical factors which have had a bearing on the present situation—a whole host of historical events and intellectual and cultural developments have contributed to the present ethical environment—several factors were chosen to be explored in depth. While the choice of religious influence does reflect the interests and the priority of values of this author, such a choice was felt justified by the almost universal recognition of the significance of these factors. Though it is difficult to measure precisely the quantitative impact of religious values on business choices, there can hardly be any doubt that they play an important role. Hence an investigation of the religious values of Protestant, Jewish, and Catholic traditions was felt to be relevant to the study of contemporary business ethics.

THE NEED FOR EMPIRICAL DATA

Nevertheless, and perhaps even more important, there is need of an empirical investigation of modern-day ethical standards of business practice. Certainly the subject of business ethics ranks among the most discussed areas in contemporary business journals. Yet one is struck by the lack of hard-core empirical data among the many valuable contributions in this area. Much of the literature in this field is based on the personal and unsystematic experience of some few authors or on generalizations from some rather infamous lapses of ethical conduct in recent years.

While conclusions based upon price-fixing cases, advertising excesses, and the like are not without some value, there is a real need for a study of an empirical nature which seeks to investigate what standards businessmen really hold. The present endeavor represents an exploratory effort in this direction.

REVIEW OF RELATED LITERATURE

Though little has been done of a scientific nature in a formal appraisal of the ethical standards of American business, some significant studies of American values and business conduct do have a relevance to the present inquiry. Hence it seems suitable to introduce the present empirical investigation with a survey of some of the more important of these contributions.

David Riesman. In a provocative study of the American character,[1] David Riesman related behavior to three ideal types: the tradition-directed, the inner-directed, and the other-directed social characters. The behavior of tradition-directed individuals is motivated by the customs and traditions of their forefathers, which have endured for centuries and have been modified but slightly, if at all, by successive generations. The inner-directed individual, on the other hand, is guided by principles and patterns of behavior implanted early in life by elders and is directed toward generalized goals which remain more or less unaltered through life. The other-directed individual looks to the approval of his contemporaries as the guide of correct behavior, and conformity to the group's norms becomes of paramount importance. Each of these types is characteristic of a society in a particular stage of population growth.

---

[1]David Riesman, The Lonely Crowd: A Study of the Changing American Character (Garden City, N.Y.: Doubleday, 1953), 359 pp.

Thus in underdeveloped countries, where there is a high potential growth rate, Riesman finds the tradition-directed social character dominant. As a country enters the transitional stage of economic growth, the inner-directed social character becomes the predominant pattern of defense against sweeping economic changes. Finally, in the stage of full economic development and incipient decline, the other-directed type predominates. Riesman sees American civilization moving toward this other-directed stage, where our values and standards consist in behavior which meets the approval of the people around us.

C. Wright Mills. C. Wright Mills[2] has launched a rather impassioned attack on the moral standards of modern society. In his The Power Elite he describes the morals of a group which certainly includes a number of top business leaders in the United States. While the study is not a strictly scientific report of empirical research, there can be little doubt that much empirical effort lies behind his investigation. His picture of business morals, especially as outlined in his final chapter, "The Higher Immorality," is a frightening one.

He sees the immorality in business not as isolated instances of irresponsible individuals, not even as evidence of corrupt administrations in certain commercial firms. Rather, as he sees it, such instances of moral breakdown tend to pull back the curtain on an institutionalized immorality—they are symptoms of a widespread condition, a condition which results from the fact that older values and codes of conduct are no longer relevant to present-day man. Nor, indeed, has man substituted a new ethic. Rather, he finds himself in a moral vacuum, where old values have lost their meaning and no new moral principles have been found to replace them. A new standard of American success—money—has become the great motivation of modern Americans. And those who have succeeded have done so because they have mastered the American system of organized irresponsibility.

W. Lloyd Warner and James C. Abegglen. Warner and Abegglen have made a more objective and more tempered study

[2]C. Wright Mills, The Power Elite (New York: The Oxford University Press, 1956).

of executive careers and executive conduct. By means of a questionnaire mailed to 7,500 business leaders and followed by a series of depth interviews, they have produced data for two important studies: Occupational Mobility[3] and Big Business Leaders in America.[4] The latter of these studies is more relevant to the present discussion, particularly the sections which explore certain aspects of executive conduct. These latter sections depend less on the data accumulated by means of the questionnaire than on depth interviews with individuals believed to manifest typical patterns of success and failure in the business world. The successful man is the one who has the personality to be mobile. To be sure, such mobility may leave him grappling with certain inconsistencies in his life, but inasmuch as he is able to adjust to the changing mores of each group in the social hierarchy as he rises on the ladder of business success, the executive himself can be successful. Indeed, if he carries with him any characteristic through his rise in corporate life, it is probably the ability to adapt to a changing physical, cultural, and moral environment. In contrast, Warner and Abegglen describe the defeated executive of the business world as one who has lost this quality of mobility. They have discovered the interesting fact that most successful men established themselves through a protege relationship with an older man, but that at a critical time the model was left behind without continuing attachment. The career pattern of the unsuccessful executive frequently reveals the inability to make this important break, which points to a lack of mobility.

Warner and Abegglen's study in some respects stands in contrast to that of Mills. The former put the decisive factor of executive success in the individual behavioral mobility; the latter views success as a function of acceptance by the in-group. But the two studies are close in another respect. They both point to an interesting question in the area of ethical conduct: Are successful executives

---

[3]W. Lloyd Warner and James C. Abegglen, Occupational Mobility in American Business and Industry (Minneapolis: University of Minnesota Press, 1955), 315 pp.

[4]W. Lloyd Warner and James C. Abegglen, Big Business Leaders in America (New York: Harper and Brothers, 1955), 243 pp.

particularly characterized by the quality of being able to accept the ethical standards of their associates? To put it another way, are businessmen characterized by a lack of deep personal ethical commitment and rather marked ability to accept group standards which may vary significantly as they rise on the executive ladder?

A. Dudley Ward. One rather sophisticated study related to the empirical survey envisaged in this study has resulted in some conclusions concerning the moral standards of American society as a whole. In 1955, A. Dudley Ward published a volume called The American Economy — Attitudes and Opinions,[5] in which he analyzes the results of a survey sponsored by the Federal Council of the Churches of Christ in America and financed by the Rockefeller Foundation. The survey consisted of questionnaires administered by qualified interviewers to 503 random residents of the Chicago area and unstructured group discussions of economic and moral attitudes in some 25 urban communities throughout the United States. There seemed to be some general agreement that United States citizens possessed a complexity of standards rather than any single or simple moral norm. Yet there was also agreement that honesty, integrity, and freedom were part of this complexus. Seven percent of the respondents, for example, acknowledged that they encountered ethical problems in connection with their work; 11 percent felt company policies to enforce ethical principles caused excessive hardships to some employees; 4 percent acknowledged that they sometimes engaged in nonethical practices; and 3 percent openly asserted that they cheated their employers.[6]

Though there was considerable discussion of specific instances of ethical problems in a variety of areas, the value of the study is somewhat limited for present purposes in that it attempts to appraise a group too heterogeneous to provide meaningful conclusions applicable to business executives. Forty-five percent of the respondents were housewives, 4 percent were employed women, 5 percent

---

[5]Alfred Dudley Ward, The American Economy — Attitudes and Opinions (New York: Harper and Brothers, 1955), 199 pp.

[6]Ibid., p. 93.

were unemployed men, and only 50 percent were men actually working full or part time. Of these latter, a large majority were employed in nonsupervisory capacities. Hence this study, while of some interest, is only peripherally related to the present investigation.

Melville Dalton. Melville Dalton's Men Who Manage[7] stands as a somewhat unique study of executive behavior in the complex atmosphere of the business firm. This detailed investigation of four midwestern companies brings to light the almost startling maneuvers of executives in their efforts to survive and rise in the corporate world. While not specifically dealing with the subject of business ethics, the study reveals an executive behavior which certainly has extensive ethical dimensions. The value of the study was greatly enhanced by the fact that much of the data was collected by means of unguarded interviews which laid bare the intrigues of corporate life. This permitted a rather comprehensive understanding of many complex situations, often involving qualitative factors which influence executive behavior but which rarely come to light in brief interviews or questionnaires. The role of conflict in executive life is clearly portrayed and is seen not only as a negative force, but also as a positive influence both in the resolution of company problems and in the development of the managerial ability of alert executives. Conflict can be the basis of the formation of cliques or power centers which permit the handling of situations that no individual leader could handle alone. But in this world of conflict it appears that the executive is kept very close to the problem of his own survival. The question may well be asked, does the executive subordinate all other values to the objective of personal survival? Are ethical standards nonoperative in a highly competitive world? Does the executive even have the choice to act ethically?

William H. Whyte. William Hollingsworth Whyte has argued, in his The Organization Man,[8] that the Protestant ethic

---

[7]Melville Dalton, Men Who Manage (New York: John Wiley and Sons, Inc. , 1959), 318 pp.

[8]William Hollingsworth Whyte, The Organization Man (New York: Simon and Schuster, 1956), 429 pp.

with its strong emphasis upon thrift, hard work, individual initiative, and independence has been replaced by a new creed: the social ethic. The new creed in many respects propounds virtues diametrically opposite to those of the Protestant ethic. This is an "outgoing" creed by which the group provides the fulfillment of the individual personality. Instead of independence, dependence is the virtue which has come into vogue. The independent man is the social isolate, a deviant who has failed to integrate with society. The dependent man has discovered his fulfillment in his sense of "belongingness" and "togetherness." So too the other extolled virtues of the Protestant ethic have been replaced by the new creed. Credit buying has replaced thrift; pension plans and social security have removed the necessity of saving; personal industry has been supplanted by the urge to prove that one "gets along well with everybody." It is more important now to integrate well with one's peers in the organization than to stand out for personal excellence or superiority.

While the modern business corporation is the vehicle used by Whyte to illustrate the evils of collective life, he sees other forms of societal life encroaching on the prerogatives of the individual: educational institutions, churches, research foundations, medical institutions, and, in brief, all parts of modern society. These organizational values put the group before the individual and demand above all else conformity to the group code or value system. Whyte is alarmed by the organization's pervasive absorption of personal individuality and suggests the only remedy to the advance of these organizational standards is a moral rejection of them by the individual and an open rebellion against the values of the Organization Man.

Richard Eells. Richard Eells,[9] in a study of the corporation, has revealed a dichotomy of value systems which has relevance to the present study. At one extreme, he sees the "traditional corporation," one which regards profit maximization as its primary if not its only objective. Such a corporation observes legal and moral prescriptions imposed by society, but in every instance its objective is to

-----

[9]Richard Eells, The Meaning of Modern Business (New York: Columbia University Press, 1960), 427 pp.

enhance the investment of the stockholders individually and collectively. At the other extreme of the social spectrum rests the metro-corporation, in which the managers view their roles as stewards for many interests, with responsibilities and objectives as diversified as the interests of the people it serves. In the middle of the spectrum Eells proposes his own model of the "well-tempered" corporation, an enterprise which is capable of adjusting to the needs of its times and to the needs of a pluralistic society which stresses such values as individual liberty, democracy, the rule of law, and the recognition of the rights of private property.

Though Eells does not describe in detail the manner in which his well-tempered organization achieves the best of two worlds, satisfying both stockholders and nonstockholder interests, his basic distinction between the traditional corporation and the metro-corporation has prompted the use of a somewhat parallel dichotomy in the ethical parameters of individual businessmen in the present study. This dichotomy will be explained more fully subsequently.

Raymond C. Baumhart. Besides these general works exploring the dimensions of values in American society, there has been one notable effort to evaluate empirically the ethical conduct of business. The Reverend Raymond C. Baumhart, S. J. , by means of a lengthy questionnaire completed by some 1,700 readers of the Harvard Business Review [10] has uncovered some interesting patterns of ethical behavior. Baumhart discovered that though businessmen tend to regard themselves as ethical, they are highly critical of the ethical performance of other businessmen. They find a wide variety of generally accepted business practices which they consider unethical. These unethical practices range from price discrimination, bribes, and excessive gift-giving to prejudice, unfairness to subordinates, and dishonesty in the making and fulfilling of contracts. More important, the Baumhart study reveals that businessmen often disagree about what is the ethical thing to do in many specific business practices. Such disagreement, while real, hides a wide area of agreement concerning basic

---

[10]Raymond C. Baumhart, S. J. , "How Ethical Are Businessmen?" Harvard Business Review, 39(4) (July-August, 1961), 6 ff.

ethical attitudes.   Baumhart concludes that executives are "alert to the social responsibilities of business as these are expressed in general terms."[11] They are also in accord with reference to the need for a general commitment to the principles of honesty and personal integrity.

DESCRIPTION OF THE METHOD USED IN THIS STUDY

PRELIMINARIES

The preceding section highlights the present state of theory in respect to the ethical motivation of business activity.   The empirical instrument designed as the basis for this part of the present study is structured on the theoretical implications of these research efforts.   (The questionnaire is found in Appendix A.) An attempt has been made to verify empirically some of the quasi-intuitive conclusions of the scholars cited above.   In those cases where empirical evidence has been proposed in support of their theses, the present effort attempts to make a specific contribution by empirically testing their conclusions among a specifically business-oriented group.   Further, use has been made of past empirical work to structure empirical findings in a more meaningful way.

Ethical Standards vs. Ethical Conduct. The questionnaire developed for this study was formulated to explore the ethical standards or ethical ideals of businessmen—this in distinction to their conduct.   Thus, unlike the Baumhart study, it purports to tell little, if anything, about "How ethical are businessmen?" There can be a wide divergence between the ethical norms of a businessman and his conduct.   Indeed, it is precisely the relationship between the ideal and the actuality which marks a man as ethical or unethical.   If the norms are lacking, then the individual may not be unethical, at least by his own standards, but rather ignorant.   Thus the content of a personal ethical creed, the recognition or lack of recognition of moral parameters by the

---

[11]Ibid., p. 10.

business executive, is the subject of the present study. Thus it cannot, and does not, aim to appraise the conduct of executives.

This distinction has a relevance to the appraisal of the veracity of the respondents' answers. While executives might be reluctant to admit to conduct which they themselves believe to be wrong, in this questionnaire they were never asked so to expose themselves. Rather, by simply indicating approval or disapproval of the cases (see section b), they revealed their standards without need of confessing any lack of conformity between their activity and these standards.

How credible are these responses, even though they do not delve into personal conduct? It would appear that in general the information is significant. There was little motive for the respondent to answer the questions more strictly than his own ethical code would call for. On the contrary, inasmuch as the respondent thought the questionnaire of value, he had every interest in being sincere in his responses, for the expressed purpose of the questionnaire was to make the standards of businessmen known rather than imposing standards from outside the business group. Even so, if there is any bias in the results, it is probably on the ethical side—i. e. , respondents may have tended to reveal higher standards in responding to the questionnaire than they really have. The questionnaire, then, may be of more value in revealing what executives consider to be clearly unethical than in revealing the total degree of moral commitment.

The Use of Cases. Several different methods were attempted in the preliminary stages of this study to determine the most suitable form with which to appraise the standards of the respondents. The final form selected was that of incident or short-case presentation. It was very early discovered that almost all executives interviewed were opposed to bribery, price-fixing, and certain other practices when presented in the abstract. When faced with concrete cases of sufficient detail so that they themselves were able to experience a certain degree of involvement, executives often answered differently. To insure that there was a sufficient grasp of the actual dilemmas faced in ethical decisions, incidents or abbreviated cases were finally chosen as the best instrument for revealing ethical standards.

The Questionnaire in General. The questionnaire was constructed with the view of using the data derived from it in several different ways. Since the objective reliability of the questionnaire is to some degree dependent upon the interpretation ascribed to the data, it is desirable at this point to explain the several uses which will be made of it.

The questionnaire reveals, first of all, certain data capable of group analysis. Thus by analysis of all the respondents' answers to the various questions of the test, it is believed that a real appreciation of the ethical commitments of the group will be manifested. This alone, it is believed, constitutes a contribution to the understanding of the present state of business morals. For while the group is not proposed as typical of the business community at large, nevertheless it does reflect the thinking of an important and influential segment of this community; and in some respects the attitudes of this group are more significant than would be a poll of the opinion of the business community in its entirety. The respondents were active businessmen participating in the Executive Training Program of the University of California at Los Angeles. [12] Members of the executive training groups are selected on the basis of their past performance in business, their ability to rise to positions above average, and their interest in furthering their own understanding of both the technical and the broader social aspects of the business profession. Undoubtedly the values of this group have more influence on business standards than do the values of the average businessman, if such an entity could be found. Thus it is believed that an appreciation of the standards of this group should be of interest; and indeed, several studies, including the Baumhart study in the Harvard Business Review, concentrate on such a general analysis of group values.

Nevertheless, it is also believed that the data of the questionnaire can reveal further insights into the standards of the individuals who responded to the questionnaire. Admittedly, such information is less reliable than predications of group results, as they involve a certain somewhat arbitrary quantification of the individual's complexus of

[12] Spring semester, 1964.

opinions. Such quantification is common to questionnaires which contain scales and scores which match responses to these scales. They are of value to the degree that their limitations are understood by those who use the results. These limitations will be explained more in detail after a description of the two scales used in the present empirical instrument.

The Parts of the Questionnaire in General. The questionnaire used in this study has been divided into four parts, each of which is related to the theoretical development of business ethics as manifested in the preceding review of literature. The first part consists of two ethical scales or indices, relating to different aspects of the executive's ethical commitments. The second part consists of a series of questions relating to the theses of Whyte and Riesman concerning the value-motivation of contemporary man. The third part of the questionnaire collects miscellaneous data which aims at revealing information relating to improvement of business ethics and also gives the respondents opportunity to reply at some length to certain aspects of their ethical convictions. The final section of the questionnaire collects demographic information important for an understanding of the character of the respondents. Each of these sections needs to be discussed in somewhat more detail.

THE PARTS OF THE QUESTIONNAIRE IN PARTICULAR

The Two Ethical Scales. These scales are based on an adaptation of Eells' models of the traditional and the well-tempered corporations. Just as it is possible for a corporation as a whole to take several different stances toward ethical problems, so is it likewise possible for the individual. These two scales, then, attempt to appraise two dimensions or two levels of ethical standards. Each scale is independent of the other in the sense that it is theoretically possible to score high on one and low on the other.

The Personal-Ethics Scale. This scale consists of eleven cases which evaluate the respondent's commitment to a specific ethical ideal. Fundamentally it is structured to judge the degree to which the respondent adheres to the values suggested by the traditional corporation.   The ideal represents an individual who believes that his ethical responsibilities are coextensive with the "rules of the game" of competition.   He has a firm commitment to personal integrity and honesty, even at the cost of personal gain.   He is further determined to obey all the laws which govern the conduct of business, regardless of personal conviction as to the usefulness of the law.   Nevertheless, when this has been done, such a person considers his ethical responsibilities fulfilled.   Beyond these commitments he is free to conduct his business as he pleases, without any danger of acting unethically.   This scale, then, manifests the degree of acceptance of two kinds of personal commitments: (a) commitment to personal integrity and honesty; and (b) commitment to the observation of laws governing business activity.

The eleven cases selected to evaluate acceptance of this ethical norm cover a variety of situations involving both legal and extralegal values.   Exhibit I (page 89) lists these and briefly describes their subject matter.

The Social Responsibility Scale.   This scale measures an ethical commitment which is different from that of the competitive norm.   It appraises the degree to which an individual considers himself ethically responsible for the social effects of business decisions: the effects of decisions on the welfare of others.   This norm considers responsibilities beyond the interest of the stockholder; and businessmen with such an ideal consider how their business decisions affect employees, customers, suppliers, and the community in which these businessmen operate.   This level of ethical commitment is measured by (a) an ethical concern for the welfare of those to whom one owes no direct legal obligation, and (b) a concern for the responsibility of business to the community as a whole.

Seven cases evaluate an executive's commitment to this index of Social Responsibility.   Exhibit II lists these and briefly describes their subject matter.

The Second Part.   The main purpose of this questionnaire has been to gather data based on responses to the cases associated with the scales just described.   All other objectives

Exhibit I

CASES: PERSONAL ETHICS SCALE

A.   Electrical-equipment price conspiracy
B.   Conflict with superior's ethics
C.   Insider information of stock split
D.   "Hard selling" of used cars
E.   Building with inferior materials
F.   Padding the expense account
G.   Promotion based on connections
H.   Pressure on newspaper by advertiser
I.   Auditor overlooks a bribe
J.   A fashion expert is hired to learn competitor's secrets
K.   Recommending questionable bonds

Exhibit II

CASES: SOCIAL-RESPONSIBILITY SCALE

A.   Electrical-equipment price conspiracy
L.   U. S. Steel and Birmingham integration
M.   Loyalty to old workers
N.   The sweatshop entrepreneur
O.   Trade with Red China
P.   Corporate donation to colleges
Q.   Graduate students as accountants

were subordinated to this goal, which was considered of primary importance. However, it was felt that the administration of the questionnaire to a rather select group of respondents presented an opportunity to gather other information without prejudicing the primary objective. The second part of the questionnaire was constructed with this objective in mind. Consequently, the results, while interesting, can be regarded only as tentative, or at best a preparatory investigation which might reveal areas of future study. Nevertheless, the results of this section were considered sufficiently significant to merit reporting in this study. Such results are not proposed as scientifically verified conclusions but as data suggestive of hypotheses for future study.

In this part five questions have been posed to the respondents in which they are asked to rank the qualities

which they feel contribute most to business success and to
ethical conduct in business. In each of the five cases, they
are asked to choose between some values which reflect the
standards of the other-directed or organizational man,
other values which reflect the ideals of the Protestant
ethic, and finally some general qualities of good managers
which reflect neither of the two value systems. These
latter qualities have been drawn from a discussion of managerial specification in one of the leading texts in management principles.[13] They are considered as incontrovertible
qualities of a good manager and were deliberately chosen
to provide the respondents with suitable alternatives to the
standards of the organizational or other-directed man, or
of the man oriented to the Protestant ethic.

The Third Part. The third part of the questionnaire proposes
to the respondents a series of questions which provides
them with the opportunity to answer at length to their
evaluation of the ethical climate of business. Three of
these questions call for answers in the form of the respondent's own expression of ethical or unethical climate
of business. Three of these questions call for answers in
the form of the respondent's own expression of ethical or
unethical conduct according to his personal experiences.
One final question in this section asks the executive to indicate degrees of approval or disapproval of a number of
suggested ways of improving the moral atmosphere of
business. In general, this part of the questionnaire reveals
qualitative rather than quantitative data; and though it might
prove difficult to present in scientific form any firm conclusion based on these data, it seemed opportune to provide
an intuitive appreciation of executive opinion with respect
to certain aspects of the present state of business morals.

The Fourth Part. The final section of the questionnaire, while
important, needs little description at this point. It is given
to the collection of demographic information concerning the
respondents. Considerable specific detail was requested
in this respect to provide for an analysis of the information

---

[13]Harold Koontz and Cyril O'Donnell, Principles of Management
(New York: McGraw-Hill Book Co., Inc., 1959), pp. 312-316.

from a wide variety of aspects. While all the information in this section was not judged to be immediately useful, nevertheless, it seemed prudent to collect it if for no other reason than to have it at hand in order to give as complete a description as possible of the test group.

THE SELECTION OF RESPONDENTS

The nature of this questionnaire presented somewhat of a unique problem regarding the selection of a suitable group to poll. The mailing of the questionnaire to a large group of respondents was likely to bring answers from those who especially regarded the subject of business ethics as important. It is highly probable that such a group would have ethical standards notably superior to those who would decline to spend the time necessary to complete the questionnaire.

As was previously mentioned, the questionnaire was administered to the members of the Executive Training Program at the University of California at Los Angeles. Since the questionnaire was administered during several of the on-campus meetings of the executive groups, the response was practically 100 percent. This was particularly fortunate in that it enabled the author to receive comments from executives who felt that the ethical climate of business was at present satisfactory and needed no improvements. In all probability, such respondents would not have taken the time to respond in such detail to a mailed questionnaire.

VALIDITY, INTERNAL CONSISTENCY, AND RELIABILITY TESTS

The formulation of this questionnaire was the result of considerable investigation which included the usual text measurements for empirical research. Five faculty members of the UCLA marketing department judged the validity of the cases used in the two scales. Next the questionnaire was submitted to a pretest. Forty-three members of the Executive Training Program participated in this pretest. The results were tabulated, and an item analysis was made of each component case in each scale. The total score of each respondent was first classified as above or below the medium score of all the respondents on the relevant scale. Then his individual response to each case was classified on the basis of approval or disapproval of the action described. Chi-square analyses of each item revealed the degree of internal consistency of the item in contributing to the total score. Such item analysis yielded a total of eighteen cases which were internally consistent. Of these items, eleven cases were relevant to the Personal-Ethics scale, and seven cases were relevant to the Social-Responsibility scale.

Several of the cases accepted scored a degree of internal consistency somewhat lower than the .10 level of confidence. This procedure was felt justified by reason of the high level of face validity of these particular cases. While this factor may cast some degree of incertitude upon the results, it was felt that such a procedure would not seriously impair the validity of the study. Rather, it seemed to suggest that the findings of the empirical study should be considered in the nature of an exploratory rather than a definitive work.

A standard test-retest reliability check was made of each of the two scales. The test was twice administered to a group of 40 subjects with a three-week interval between test administrations. The test-retest reliability coefficient for the personal ethics scale was .76. While this coefficient is somewhat on the low side, it still manifests an acceptable degree of reliability. The test-retest reliability coefficient for the social-responsibility scale was .86, which reveals a high degree of reliability.

The difficulties involved in the preliminary phases of this questionnaire are set forth candidly so that the limitations of the study may be clearly understood. Quite frankly, this researcher was aware that these preliminary steps involved a degree of compromise. The construction of a rigidly defensible empirical tool which would result in scientifically incontestable results would have demanded time and resources beyond the means of this researcher. At the same time, an effort was made to adhere as closely as possible to standards which would make the study significant. It is believed that the study does make a contribution to the understanding of ethical values of business executives, provided that the results are interpreted in the light

of the limitations just explained, and provided that definitive generalizations are carefully avoided.

SUMMARY OF THE CHAPTER

This chapter is preliminary in nature and serves as an
introduction to the empirical section of the study. After
explaining the need for empirical research in the area of
ethical standards of business, a survey of relevant literature was presented. Attention was then given to a consideration of the questionnaire itself in the belief that such
information was vital to an appreciation of both its strengths
and its weaknesses. The structure of the questionnaire
was explained in detail, and then a description of the preliminary stages of judging and pretesting was given. It is
believed that while the questionnaire manifests certain
deficiencies which are the result of compromise with ideal
standards of scientific inquiry and practical problems of
limited resources, the results, when considered in the light
of the inherent limitations as described, do contribute to
a deeper appreciation of the actual ethical standards of
businessmen.

Chapter 5

RESULTS OF THE QUESTIONNAIRE: PART I

INTRODUCTION

The present chapter and the next are directed to the description and interpretation of the results of the questionnaire. These results will be considered in detail in order that their significance and limitations can be clearly understood.

In the preceding chapter it was noted that the data derived from the questionnaire can be viewed from several viewpoints. First, the data can be considered in the light of group analysis. Though the executives do not represent a group which is typical of American businessmen, nevertheless, they do seem to have characteristics in common with an important segment of the business community. Without any attempt to generalize from the responses of the group to the opinion of the business community as a whole, the results have a relevance and an interest which warrant a discussion of the group's commitments to the ethical values implied in the various parts of the questionnaire. This chapter will be directed to the study of group data along these lines.

The next chapter will be devoted to the consideration of the scales which have been embodied in the case section of the questionnaire. As was explained above, this information seems of less scientific worth than the basic analysis of the group responses to each of the questions. Nevertheless, it seems of sufficient value to merit a detailed exposition and should be of significance if interpreted in the light of the limitations which are implied in its structure.

THE EXECUTIVE PROFILE

Exhibit III gives a brief summary of the more important demographic characteristics of the group. It will be observed that the group as a whole appears to be rather young relative to the positions which they hold in business. The median age was in the 40-44 year bracket, and at the same time 44 percent held positions which they classified as top-management level. Only 14 percent of the respondents viewed their jobs as below the middle-management level, though another 3 percent classified themselves as professionals. These figures highlight the fact that the group is atypical in the sense that they seem to manifest a degree of success above average, especially in comparison with other executives in similar age brackets.

A sizeable majority (68 percent) described themselves as Protestants. An attempt was made to make this information more specific. The questionnaire asked Protestants to indicate their specific denominations. It was hoped that by classifying these denominations into two groups, those influenced by Calvinism and those which were non-Calvinistic, the impact of the Protestant ethic could be investigated in more detail. This effort must be regarded as a failure. Only about one fourth (eighteen) of the Protestants indicated their specific denominations. Of these, only seven were members of non-Calvinistic faiths. It was felt that no general conclusions could be made from such a small sample, and the attempt to compare adherence to the Protestant ethic among Calvinists and non-Calvinists was abandoned. This decision was confirmed by discussion with several religious leaders who questioned the validity of a clear-cut distinction between Calvinist and non-Calvinist denominations. It was their belief that the Calvinist doctrine has influenced many faiths in varying degrees so that such a dichotomy would be nearly meaningless.

Data relating to income seem more reliable when salary is considered alone than when total income is used as a criterion. Consequently, the total income data have not been included in this report. All but 4 percent of the respondents seemed willing to specify the income derived from their salaries. But over 21 percent declined to specify their total income from all sources. Though assurances were given to the executives that their responses

Exhibit III

THE TEST GROUP: DEMOGRAPHIC INFORMATION

1. Age:

	Number
Under 30 years	0
30 - 34	8
35 - 39	21
40 - 44	35
45 - 49	25
50 - 54	7
55 - 59	4
60 - 65	0
Over 65 years	0
No answer	3
Total	103

2. Religion:

	Number
Protestant	70
Catholic	12
Jewish	9
Other	2
None	7
No answer	3
Total	103

3. Position:*

	Number
Top management	44
Middle management	39
Frontline supervisory position	14
Nonmanagement personnel	0
Professional	3
No answer	3
Total	103

4. Formal Education:

	Number
High school or less	5
Some college	18
Bachelor's degree	26
Some graduate studies	31
M.A., M.B.A., or higher	21
No answer	2
Total	103

5. Income from salary:

	Number
less than $5,000	0
$ 5,000 - $ 7,499	0
7,500 - 9,999	1
10,000 - 14,999	11
15,000 - 19,999	27
20,000 - 24,999	29
25,000 - 29,999	15
30,000 - 39,999	14
40,000 - 49,999	1
50,000 - 59,999	1
60,000 or over	0
No answer	4
Total	103

*See questionnaire, Appendix A, for definition of these terms.

would be anonymous, and although they were not asked to give their names, the identities of the participants could be discovered from the information contained in the demographic section of the questionnaire.   No attempt was made to use the questionnaire in such a manner, but the fact that such identification is possible may account for the reluctance of the respondents to give precise information relating to their total income.   It must be admitted that some of the demographic information requested was of a highly personal nature.   Yet the completeness of the responses and the cooperation of the participants was one of the most satisfying aspects of the research experience.

In another respect the respondents manifest themselves as atypical.   Only 5 percent admitted of no amount of college education.   This is a very low figure indeed; and since over 50 percent of the respondents indicated the name of the last school they attended, there is indication that this datum is reliable.   It is, of course, more or less expected. The academic content of the Executive Training Program is quite sophisticated, and probably would be less attractive and less meaningful to those with deficient educational backgrounds.   Over 50 percent of the respondents indicated that they had some graduate studies, and 20 percent attested to the fact that they had been awarded a graduate degree.

Thus, while the demographic data give evidence that the respondents to the questionnaire are not a typical group, they do seem to be an influential group in American business.   And while generalizations need to be avoided in the appraisal of their opinions, nevertheless, an understanding of their ethical standards and their ethical commitments should prove of considerable value.

THE EXECUTIVE SPEAKS ON ETHICS

THE CASES

The Cases in General. How did the executives judge the moral issues in the cases of the questionnaire?   Exhibit IV gives in collective form this information.   The executives responded to each of the cases by indicating degrees of approval or disapproval along a five-point scale.   In the

Exhibit IV

HOW THE EXECUTIVES ANSWERED THE CASES

Letter	Description of Case**	Percent				
		1*	2*	3*	4*	5*
A	Electrical-equipment price fixing	3	18	0	14	65
B	Conflict with superior's ethics	15	12	0	31	42
C	Use of insider information	30	18	0	15	37
D	Sharp selling of used cars	7	7	0	21	65
E	Use of inferior materials	3	4	0	9	84
F	Padding the expense account	2	5	0	18	75
G	Promotion of less capable	7	9	0	15	69
H	Advertising influence with newspaper	12	25	0	24	39
I	Auditor's report conceals bribe	18	24	0	21	37
J	Pirating employee to learn competitor's secrets	18	22	0	20	40
K	Recommending inferior bonds	7	10	0	29	54
L	U.S. Steel's refusal to exert pressure for racial integration	73	12	0	7	8
M	Discharge of older workers	10	26	0	28	36
N	"Sweatshop" entrepreneur	28	31	0	19	22
O	Trading with Red China	33	10	0	11	46
P	Corporate contribution to colleges	13	8	0	12	67
Q	Foreign students as accounting apprentices	67	15	0	10	8
R	Expensive Christmas gifts	22	18	1	25	34
S	Campaign contribution for a contract	4	8	0	18	70
T	Costly chemical filter	3	1	0	4	92
U	Trucking firm with captive customer	19	10	0	17	54
V	Hiding plant shutdown from employees	7	2	0	10	81
W	Executive's community activities	2	3	0	14	81
X	Objectionable television program	12	7	0	26	55
Y	Fair return over profit-maximization	8	9	1	7	75
Z	Selling speculative land	34	20	2	20	24

*See the text, p. 99, for the interpretation of these numbers.
**See Appendix A, pp. 178 and following, for the cases.

construction of the cases, care was given that approval of the proposed "solutions" would not consistently be in the same direction, i. e. , toward support of social values over personal gain. In a number of cases, approval of the solution proposed in the case itself represented a choice of personal gain over social values. Therefore, the answers of these latter cases needed to be inverted in order that the responses as they appear in Exhibit IV might have a common interpretation. This has been done. As the alternatives appear, the answers one through five have the following meanings:

1. An unequivocal choice of profit or personal advantage over an ethical value or social goal.

2. A reserved choice of profit or personal advantage over an ethical value or social goal.

3. No opinion (expressed by no indicated response to the case).

4. A reserved choice of an ethical value or social goal over profit or personal advantage.

5. An unequivocal choice of an ethical value or social goal over profit or personal advantage.

It must be noted that an answer of one or two does not necessarily imply approval of unethical conduct. As explained earlier, the questionnaire is not designed to determine whether or not the executives are "ethical" or "unethical. " Such an objective would imply that there was already a commonly accepted and sharply defined code to which individual standards could be compared. Such a code does not exist, at least in many points of specific application, and in its absence to interpret these responses as ethical or unethical would imply the use of one's own code as an absolute. In order to avoid the use of such subjective criteria, the responses are interpreted simply as indicating whether or not a specific act is approved or disapproved of by the respondent's own personal codes. Thus the questionnaire is an exploratory study of the dimensions of executive standards, and aims at no more than determining whether or not specific cases are related to these standards.

Exhibit IV reveals several striking characteristics of the respondents' value systems. First of all, there seems to be a wide difference of opinion with respect to the direction of the ethical response. In only eight of the twenty-six cases was there an 80 percent agreement concerning such direction, and in only six of these cases was agreement above the 90 percent level. Thus, even apart from consideration of the firmness of commitment, the executives manifested sharp differences of opinions with respect to their ethical evaluation of some rather common situations in the business environment. This result seems to confirm with respect to the present group one of the conclusions of the Baumhart study: that there is no commonly accepted ethical standard among executives today. [1]

Another fact readily observable from an analysis of Exhibit IV is related to the extension of the respondents' opinions with respect to ethical values. The instructions read at the beginning of the test sessions asked the participants to make a sincere effort to answer each question, but if they were unable to make a decision or if they had no opinion with respect to any given case, to leave the question blank. In over 2,600 responses involved in this section of the questionnaire, only four "no opinion" or "don't know" votes were recorded. This is considered an extraordinarily high percentage of response and seems to indicate that executives do have value systems which are related to the wide variety of concrete business problems.

The firmness of the executives' ethical convictions is another matter. Of the five choices given the executives (including the choice of not answering), two reflected some degree of hesitance or incertitude on the part of the respondents. Approximately 30 percent of the responses were in this category. Thus the executives were slow to give unreserved answers with respect to the application of moral values to concrete business situations. To some degree this incertitude might point to the fact that the executives were of the opinion that not enough information was given to warrant a firm commitment; and, indeed, some three or four instances occurred where the participants indicated such was the case by comment on the

---

[1] Raymond C. Baumhart, S. J., "How Ethical are Businessmen?" Harvard Business Review, 39 (July-August, 1961), p. 9.

questionnaire.   Nevertheless, it is felt that the major
source of hesitancy goes deeper than this and points to the
difficulty of applying value systems to concrete business
conditions.   Indeed, a number of executives remarked that
this was precisely where they found the questionnaire most
difficult.

The Cases Discussed Individually. Much of the information revealed by the questionnaire can be appreciated only by
means of a detailed discussion of the cases.   Accordingly,
the present section analyzes the responses of the executives to each of the cases and tentatively suggests motivations which might have been operative in the opinions these
respondents expressed.   Emphasis needs to be put on the
tentative nature of the following pages: these pages represent an effort to suggest the complex pattern of motives
which may underlie executive choices.   Consequently, the
following analysis can provide valuable insights only if its
speculative nature is kept in mind.

In the formative stages of the questionnaire, it was
suggested that the first case (Case A), involving the electrical-equipment price-fixing conspiracy of 1960, would be
unsuitable inasmuch as most executive thinking had been
influenced by the generally hostile accounts of the incident
in the press.   Yet a full 21 percent of the respondents expressed some degree of approval of the action of the convicted executives, though a large percentage of these were
not willing to give more than reserved approval. In search-
ing for an explanation of this response, several factors
need to be considered. Undoubtedly there was considerable
pressure brought to bear on these executives, both by their
own superiors and by the seriousness of the chaotic pricing
conditions which prevailed from time to time when the gen-
tleman's agreement was temporarily or partially abandoned.   Such freely moving prices were so disruptive that
satisfactory managerial performance was in practice impossible, and as a result the personal survival of the
executives became a decisive issue.   Thus the sizable minority who approved of the executives' illegal action could
have been reflecting a sympathetic attitude toward the
pressures the aforementioned executives were facing.

Another motivating factor might have had a relevance
in this response.   In spite of public support of antitrust

philosophy and an almost unqualified belief in the value of competition, executives also seem to value highly an "orderly" market condition. Indeed, they see this orderly market condition as a useful means of providing the community with a maximum contribution from the business sector. While this value seems to conflict with the traditional concept of competition, apparently this inconsistency did not bother at least some of the executives. Robert N. McMurry [2] has discussed this phenomenon and has suggested that it offers some promise in the direction of resolving conflicts of standards among various individuals. More immediately, it would seem at least some of the 21 percent who approved of price-fixing tactics were not simply condoning illegal activity but were grappling with a difficult conflict between two values. They may not be as "unethical" as the response may make them first appear to be. This is especially true when it is considered that only 14 percent of those who approved of the price-fixing activities were unqualified in their approval.

In Case B a sizable minority (27 percent) of respondents expressed approval of the action of a sales representative who followed a sales policy which he considered unethical. This response is at first glance surprising, for these executives seem to be suggesting that an individual can set aside the dictates of his own conscience when these stand in the way of the fulfillment of his superior's orders. Yet this response may do no more than reflect the executives' attitude that many issues of business ethics are best described as areas of grey, areas where absolutes and certainties are rare. The uncertainty factor in moral decisions is evidently high, and the application of broad principles to specific circumstances demands a considerable amount of judgment. In the case cited, there is an expressed difference of opinion between the sales representative and his superior concerning the moral quality of a new sales policy. In such cases a number of the 27 percent approving the action of the sales representative may have been motivated by the belief that in areas of doubt, the executive can morally follow the opinion of another

---

[2] Robert N. McMurry, "Conflicts in Human Values," Harvard Business Review, XLI (May-June, 1963), 130 ff.

responsible person.   If this is not the case, and these executives really believe that they may substitute the command of a superior for their own moral responsibility, they are dangerously approaching the position of the Nazi war criminals at the 1945 and 1946 Nuremberg trials.

Another interesting and somewhat surprising result occurred with respect to Case C, which dealt with the use of insider information for personal gain, a practice clearly prohibited by Securities and Exchange Commission regulations.   Nearly one half of the respondents (48 percent) expressed approval of the use of such information for personal advantage, and most of these latter were firm in their opinion.   It is true that the case presents a situation in which the cost of refusing to use this information is very high: personal bankruptcy.   But in a business environment which so clearly and forcefully prohibits such activity, it seems somewhat startling that so many respondents would be willing to disregard society's judgment of such activity. It is hard to judge the motives of the respondents who approved of this illegal use of insider information.   It may be that they fail to see a damage done to society by such an action comparable to the harm which the board member himself would incur if he refrained from such action, or that they are inclined to discount the distant ill effect to society in favor of the immediate welfare of the director.

In Case D a large percentage of the executives (86 percent) took exception to what may be regarded as common practices in used-car merchandising.   Such practices, as listed in the case, included deliberate deception and pressure tactics.   Apparently the respondents have little difficulty in judging such actions as reprehensible.   In another case, an impressive majority (93 percent) frowned upon the use of inferior materials in the fulfillment of a business contract (Case E).   And in a similar case, the testees strongly rejected the action of a construction-company executive who made a large campaign contribution in order to receive a contract to build a new city hall (Case S).   Both these cases manifest a keen sensitivity to the moral parameters at stake in contract relationships.   It is believed that this interesting result may reflect the involvement of this particular test group with contract work.   A good percentage of the respondents is connected with either construction companies or companies heavily committed to defense work. In both of these types of concerns, contract relationships are fundamental to the well-being and even the survival of the businesses.

A similarly large majority (93 percent) expressed disapproval of the practice of padding an expense account (Case F). This is an especially interesting result inasmuch as these respondents seem to take strong exception to what is apparently a somewhat widespread practice. It is believed that the factor which motivated this response was the fact that the salesman in question seemed to have a well-thought-out and deliberate pattern of supplementing his annual income 5 percent by expense-account spending. This is something far more questionable than an occasional decision to exaggerate expenses to some small degree or to charge an occasional nonauthorized expenditure to the account. It may also be that this case touches an area which is so frequently discussed in connection with business ethics that the respondents have come to recognize it as fundamentally wrong. This latter explanation opens the door to speculation concerning the influence of educational processes on business standards and suggests the possibility of raising such standards through formal study. At any rate, Cases D, E, and F, as well as several other cases to be discussed later, reveal that there is some community of opinion in the ethical standards of the respondents. In at least a few areas, ethical problems seem sufficiently clear-cut to form the basis of some generally accepted principles of business ethics.

A somewhat unexpected response was recorded in reference to a case dealing with the promotion of the less capable of two executives on the basis of family connections (Case G). In the formative stages of the questionnaire it was suggested that there would be almost universal approval of the promotion and that to make the case more balanced the opportunities of the executive not promoted should be sharply restricted. This was done. The result was that 84 percent of the respondents disapproved of this promotion, even though it was clearly in the interests of the company. Unfortunately, it must be admitted that the present research does not shed much light on the reason for such strong expression of disapproval. The respondents may have felt that an injustice was done to the executive not promoted. On the other hand, they may simply have felt that the long-range benefit of the company was furthered more by the promotion of the less-qualified individual.   The questions asked in personal interviews failed to clarify the reasoning of the respondents in this respect, and little can be definitely inferred from the response.

In another case (Case H) 37 percent of the test group found no need to disapprove of the pressures exerted by an advertiser to suppress an unfavorable news item about his store.   Since the item was of small moment, some executives probably regarded the suppression of the news as a small favor which did no harm to the public welfare.   Businessmen have learned to work through the exchange of favors and ordinarily accept such acts as part of the realities of the business world.   Nevertheless, 63 percent of the respondents took exception to the practice.   Clearly, there is a substantial degree of disagreement on this case; it may be that the majority look upon the newspaper's obligation to publish such news as related to its public trust.

In another case (Case I) the respondents again divided sharply on the responsibility to follow the literal interpretations of the law.   Some 42 percent of the respondents approved of an auditor's decision to overlook a bribe which was forced upon a trucking company by a dishonest union official.   Another 21 percent only "somewhat disapproved" of the auditor's decision.   Thus it would seem that the executives felt that the law does not always give unequivocal solutions to ethical dilemmas.   On the contrary, they seem of the opinion that there is need of human judgment of the circumstances surrounding each specific case in order to arrive at ethically correct decisions.   In their minds, legal codes do not substitute for the necessity of human judgment.

The test group was again sharply divided over the problem of employee pirating for the purpose of obtaining trade secrets (Case J). A full 40 percent of the respondents leaned toward approval of this action.   Perhaps they were motivated by a high regard for the competitive system, for which a certain mobility of labor and price competition is a prerequisite.   Certainly there is no legal proscription of such activity, and in the absence of such prohibition they may regard the practice as within the accepted bounds of competitive activity.

A full 73 percent of the respondents disapproved of a salesman in an investment house recommending bonds of questionable quality (Case K). Apparently these executives are quick to recognize the professional relationship that exists between an investment counselor and his client, and they strongly reprove the use of this privileged relationship in a way which compromises the interests of the client.

In Case L, 85 percent of the test group approved of a statement by Roger Blough to the effect that a corporation should not use economic coercion to achieve social goals. This seems to indicate that a majority find such activity as beyond the legitimate scope of corporate activity. The question points to a degree of social concern and involvement which is clearly beyond what these executives consider proper. It is probably fair to conclude that these men feel that the corporation, while responding to social norms, should commit itself to objectives which are more profit-centered or at least more economic in character.

The responses to Case Q seem to reflect the same kind of value judgments. In this case, 82 percent approved of the decision of an accounting firm not to accept a number of foreign students as summer trainees. The decision was made on the basis of incompatibility with company efficiency, and the approval of this decision by a large majority of the test group once again seems to point to the limits to which the respondents are willing to subordinate profit objectives to general social goals.

At the same time, a series of cases reveals that the executives do recognize in principle the need to subordinate on some occasions profit maximization to social goals. Case W concerns an executive's decision to devote some of his company time to community projects even though these projects did not ostensibly contribute to corporate objectives. Ninety-five percent of the respondents approved of this decision, indicating that there is a wide consensus that some such community activity is commendable. In a similar case (Case T), 96 percent approved of the installation of a costly chemical-filter system which reduced the net income of an oil refinery for several years, though no ordinance compelled such installation. In Case V, 91 percent disapproved of concealing from employees a plant shutdown; and again in Case Y, 82 percent approved of General Motors' postwar pricing policy based on fair-return rather than profit-maximization objectives. On the other hand, in other cases involving the sacrifice of personal or corporate gain for social goals, the respondents are much more divided.   In Cases M, N, O, and P only a slim majority favor such subordination of profit maximization, and a substantial minority choose to place responsibility for corporate economic goals above other social goals.   Thus it seems that these cases point to a complex value structure in regard to this area, and this pattern will be analyzed more carefully in a subsequent chapter.

With respect to one highly criticized corporate practice, the exchange of expensive Christmas gifts, the respondents are more hesitant to see the issue as a clear-cut case of bribery than was anticipated by this writer (Case R).   The executives split rather sharply in their evaluation of the ethical implications of such gifts, with about 40 percent expressing a willingness to go along with the practice where it is long established. Apparently they are motivated by the conviction that large gifts do not necessarily imply moral suasion to practice favoritism.   However, with the respondents so closely divided, it is difficult to draw any strong inferences concerning motivations in this case.

Two cases (Cases U and X) reveal interesting patterns of executive opinion.   In the first of these cases, 71 percent of the respondents objected to the formation of a trucking company which would enjoy special privileges in servicing certain captive customers.   Apparently this majority felt such private "cornering of the market" is incompatible with the competitive system which the vast majority support.   In the second of the cases above, a full 81 percent took exception to the remark of a television executive that his company had as an objective the marketing of a popular product and need not be concerned with an attempt to upgrade the moral values of society.   It may be that the respondents reject the absoluteness of the disassociation with values.   Perhaps a somewhat more balanced expression of the relationship between economic goals of the corporation and the social values of the community would have been more acceptable.

The final case (Case Z) revealed a somewhat unexpected result as the majority of the respondents (54 percent) approved the tactics of certain real estate speculators who sold desert lots by mail.   In expressing this opinion the executives probably felt there is a present-day relevancy to the age-old adage "Caveat emptor." If no positive misinformation is contained in the promotional material (a supposition of the case), then the buyer himself has a certain responsibility in deciding for himself the merits of the speculative risk. This was an opinion expressed in several interviews related to the questionnaire.

Case Comparisons. Some interesting light can be shed upon executive standards by comparing the responses of individual cases with one another. Exhibit V lists the cases in a manner which facilitates such an analysis. The cases are arranged in an order which reflects the respondents' increasing acceptance of social values at the sacrifice of personal or corporate gain. Cases at the top of Exhibit V are those in which only a small minority of the executives are willing to sacrifice personal or corporate gain for social values. As the cases are listed one after another, a greater percentage of the executives accept the social value exemplified by the case at the cost of personal gain. At the end of the exhibit are listed those cases in which there is an almost unanimous agreement that personal gain must be subordinated to social goals in the particular circumstances embodied in the case presentation.

Such an organization of executive responses reveals interesting information concerning the subject matter of the cases in reference to the firmness of executive opinion. In order to make these data more meaningful, the cases have been classified into four areas which are characterized by a similarity of firmness of executive opinion. These areas have been called the Area of Strong Opposition, the Area of Balanced Disagreement, the Area of Relative Agreement, and, finally, the Area of Proximate Unanimity. It is hoped that by comparing certain cases with one another in reference to their position in one of these four areas, certain new insights to executive standards will be revealed.

Cases V and N. Ninety-one percent of the respondents disapproved of hiding a plant shutdown from employees who would be left jobless by the shutdown (Case V). This case clearly qualifies as within the Area of Relative Agreement. However, these same respondents revealed substantial disagreement concerning the practice of the

Exhibit V

CASE COMPARISONS

Letter	Description of Case	Percent Choosing Social Value	Classifi-cation
L	U.S. Steel's refusal to exert pressure for racial integration	15	Area of Strong Opposition
M	Foreign students as accounting apprentices	18	
N	"Sweatshop" entrepreneur	41	
Z	Selling speculative land	46	
C	Use of insider information	52	
O	Trading with Red China	57	
I	Auditor's report conceals a bribe	58	Area of Balanced Disagree-ment
J	Pirating an employee to learn competitor's secrets	60	
R	Expensive Christmas gifts	60	
B	Conflict with superior's ethics	63	
H	Advertiser influence with newspaper	63	
M	Discharge of older workers	64	

(continued)

Exhibit V (continued)

Letter	Description of Case	Percent Choosing Social Value	Classifi- cation
U	Trucking firm with captive customer	71	
A	Electrical-equipment price fixing	79	
P	Corporate contribution to colleges	79	
X	Objectionable television program	81	
K	Recommending inferior bonds	83	
Y	Fair return over profit maximization	83	Area of
G	Promotion of less capable executive	84	Relative Agreement
D	Sharp selling of used cars	86	
S	Campaign contribution for a contract	88	
V	Hiding plant shutdown from employees	91	
E	Use of inferior materials	93	
F	Padding the expense account	93	
W	Executive's community activities	95	Area of Proximate
T	Costly chemical filter	96	Unanimity

entrepreneur who imposed upon his employees substandard working conditions (Case N). Fifty-nine percent of the respondents at least somewhat approved of this action, while 41 percent thought the practice wrong. This reveals an interesting dichotomy in executive standards toward employee relations. Apparently the respondents felt more keenly about the obligation of an employer to be concerned with the continued employment of his employees than with their working conditions. It may well be that this interesting distinction in employer obligations is based on a recognition of the importance of employment for personal economic survival in a modern economy.

Cases J and G. A parallel set of cases reveals an interesting standard in reference to company employees of executive rank. Case J exhibits a marked difference of opinion concerning the hiring of the manager of a competitor's plant in order to learn trade secrets. The respondents divided sharply on the propriety of such tactics, with 60 percent approving the practice, 40 percent disapproving. In another case dealing with an executive employee (Case G), 84 percent disapproved of a decision to promote a less capable executive because he had family connections with his firm's largest customer. It may be that this pattern of response points to a sensitivity which is more alert to standards of executive appraisal after they have been employed by a company than to the appraisal standards of the hiring process. Performance seems to be the decisive criterion in the estimation or promotability. The respondents are more willing to accept extrinsic advantage to the firm as motivation for hiring. Thus there seems to be expressed in this pattern of response a belief that executives may be hired for sundry reasons, but once associated with a company, ability and performance should be the criteria for advancement.

Cases R and S. Case R concerns an executive who sends expensive Christmas gifts to company customers, even though he feels this compromises their position as buyers and exerts pressure on them to practice favoritism in placing orders. The case definitely falls within the Area of Balanced Disagreement. Sixty percent of the respondents disapproved of this practice, but 40 percent found no reason

for such disapproval. In a somewhat similar case, the respondents took a different stance. A full 88 percent disapproved the action of a construction company executive who
made a campaign contribution to a local politician in exchange for a contract to build a new city hall (Case S).
This reveals an interesting distinction which the respondents see in the two cases. It may be that the decisive factor
in the first case which led to the substantial difference of
opinion was the fact that the practice of exchanging expensive gifts was described as commonly practiced by the
whole industry. The case of the campaign contribution was
clearly not justified by an industry-wide custom or practice. If this was the actual motive for the respondents'
distinction between the issues involved in the two cases, it
highlights the importance these men place upon the circumstances and the environment which surround moral
decisions.

Cases Z and D. The executives were almost evenly
divided in their evaluation of a case which involved selling
speculative desert land through mass-media promotion
(Case Z). Fifty-four percent of the respondents approved
of this practice, while 46 percent disapproved. Clearly
this case falls within the Area of Balanced Disagreement.
But another case involving a questionable sales policy finds
the same respondents in relative agreement (Case D).
Eighty-six percent of the executives took exception to the
selling tactics of a used-car salesman who set back the
speedometers, superficially hid major defects of his cars,
and attempted to apply various types of pressure to force
prospective customers into an early commitment to purchase a car. A comparison of these two cases seems to
indicate that the respondents draw a rather sharp line between acceptable and unacceptable sales practices. In the
first case, while the real estate promoters did use forceful
promotion tactics to market their desert lots, they did not
engage in positive deception. In the case of the used-car
salesman, such fraudulent methods were used, and apparently it is for this reason that a strong majority of the
respondents disapproved of the latter case.

Cases C and K. An interesting diversity of standards shows up in connection with two cases which imply a

"trust" or professional-client relationship. The respondents were in relative disagreement in their appraisal of the
conduct of a corporation director who used insider information for personal gain (Case C). Fifty-two percent of
the test group disapproved of this action, but an almost
equal proportion, 48 percent, found no conflict between this
conduct and their own value standards. However, in another case involving a professional relationship, 83 percent
disapproved of a bond salesman who recommended to customers questionable bonds in order to reduce his company's
inventory in these bonds (Case K). Several factors may
have contributed to this interesting dichotomy with respect
to fiduciary relationships. The first of these two cases
seems to imply less of a professional relationship than
does the latter. While a corporation director does act as a
trustee of the stockholders, this relationship traditionally
seems to be regarded as less restrictive than that of an
investment broker with his client. If this is so, then it may
be that the test group is making this interesting distinction
on the basis of the strictness of the fiduciary relationship.

On the other hand, there is another interesting factor
which may have influenced a substantial variance in these
responses. While in both cases the fiduciary agent seems
to be using his professional relationship for personal gain,
in the first case there is no positive act of deception on the
part of the corporation director. He is simply making use
of information which is not generally available. In the second of these cases, the circumstances in this respect are
quite different. The bond salesman is engaging in some
degree of positive deception by recommending a bond which
he does not really consider worthy of such confidence. And
his client is taken advantage of by such deception. This
distinction is a fine one, but one which cannot be entirely
discounted in attempting to understand the significance of
the responses to these two cases.

Cases M and V. In two other cases the test group
manifests an interesting difference of opinion in reference
to the treatment of employees in the face of a plant shutdown. Case M describes a situation in which an employer
facing the necessity of closing one of his plants discharges
his older and more highly paid workers while transferring
the younger workers to another plant. Only 64 percent of

the respondents disapproved of this treatment—a clear but relatively small majority when compared with Case V. In this latter instance 91 percent of the respondents objected to the decision of management to keep secret from employees an imminent plant shutdown.

Case V is solidly in the Area of Relative Agreement, while Case M reveals considerable difference of opinion in the respondents' judgment. It is hard to account for the distinction which the respondents make between the two cases. It may be that in Case V, the executives reasoned that some of the employees had to be discharged under any circumstance and that management could distribute the discharge in such a way as to make the company more competitive in the future. In Case M, on the contrary, the concealing of the plant shutdown imposed an avoidable wrong on the employees. If such is the reasoning behind the distinction made in these two cases, the responses point to a norm operative in the thinking of at least some of the respondents: management should avoid action which will be clearly detrimental to employees; but when the harm is unavoidable, it may be distributed with a view to the best interests of the company.

Cases S and E. A small group of cases is of particular interest because of their supporting, rather than conflicting, character. Cases S and E are in this group. Both of these cases deal with contract relationships, and in each of the cases the respondents support a stance of fairness and integrity which extends to both the making and fulfilling of contract commitments. In Case S, 88 percent of the test group objected to the decision of a construction contractor to make a political campaign contribution in exchange for a contract to build a new city hall. In Case E, an even larger majority disapproved of a low contract bid which was made with the intention of using inferior materials to permit a suitable profit margin. Clearly this particular group of executives have a keen sense of propriety in respect to the ethical dimensions of contract relationships.

Cases W and T. The two cases which are found in the Area of Proximate Unanimity both point to an acceptance by the test group of management's responsibility for noneconomic goals of society even at the cost of decreased profits. Case W concerns a corporation president who commits some of his time to community-sponsored activities and recommends the same to his subordinates. Ninety-five percent of the executives supported this position. In Case T, an oil refinery installed an expensive filter system to cut down on soot and odor which affected nearby housing tracts. Ninety-six percent of the test group approved of this action, even though it was expressly stated that the new filter system would noticeably reduce net income for several years. Thus the test group seems to support overwhelmingly the rights of managers to sacrifice some profits for social goals.

Cases L and Q. On the other hand, the test group is almost equally emphatic in supporting the right of executives to reject such noneconomic goals when these goals seem to interfere fundamentally with company objectives. In Cases L and Q, which make up the Area of Strong Opposition, a large majority of the respondents support managers in this kind of decision. Eighty-one percent of the test group approved the decision of the head of a public accounting firm to refuse a request to accept foreign students as apprentice accountants with the firm. In Case L, an even greater majority (85 percent) agreed with a statement of Roger Blough that a corporation should not attempt to exercise economic compulsion or pressure to achieve noneconomic or social goals. Thus, while the respondents do support an executive's right to be concerned with other goals besides profit maximization, they are almost equally firm in their support of the right of an executive to make decisions by means of a profit-maximization calculus. And in those instances in which social goals conflict with the firm's economic objectives, the respondents tend to reflect the opinion that the business executive is in the best position to balance such conflicting goals.

Summary. In summary we have a composite picture of executives who show a keen interest in the ethical dimensions of business decisions. They are strongly committed to ideals of honesty, integrity, and fair play, though they differ widely in their application of these qualities to concrete situations. In most of the cases presented, they found themselves rather sure of their own ethical evaluation, but in a significant number of instances they are reluctant to give an unequivocal answer. They manifest an appreciation of the role of law in regulating and guiding business, but feel that the individual needs to judge the relevance of the law to specific applications. They give expression to the opinion that business has social responsibilities which are not completely satisfied with an unmitigated commitment to profit maximization, indeed, sometimes even conflict with profit maximization. At the same time they retain a practical respect and appreciation of the legitimacy of the profit motive. In brief, they are a group of men with complex and sometimes even conflicting values, and they defy any attempt to classify them into simple, clear-cut categories.

THE RANKING QUESTIONS: THE ORGANIZATION MAN vs. THE PROTESTANT ETHIC

The second part of the questionnaire consisted of five questions which asked the respondents to rank qualities which they consider important for business success, or qualities which they would like to find in their associates. Twenty-three rankings were requested from the respondents, though some of these represent a repetition of the same qualities vis-à-vis a different set of alternatives. As was indicated in the previous chapter, there is a reluctance upon the part of this researcher to interpret the results of this and the following sections in an absolute manner as this aspect of the research was definitely subordinated to objectives related to the cases. Nevertheless, the results of the questions are of sufficient interest to warrant consideration here, and if not of strict scientific value, may serve as an exploratory effort which gives some clue of executive commitment to well-defined value patterns.

Exhibit VI reveals the collective opinion of the executives in ranking these qualities. The results are presented in the form of an average ranking for each quality. The first group (questions 31-35) asks the executives to rank the qualities as they consider them desirable traits in their associates. Two of the qualities in this first group represent the traditional virtues of the Protestant ethic (hard work and thrift). One other quality reflects the values of the organization man (ability to get along with others). Two final qualities were inserted as "neutral" values, one which did not immediately reflect one or the other of these value systems (leadership and technical know-how). The results of the respondents' rankings were somewhat surprising. Except for the quality of thrift, which clearly scored least desirable in the executives' opinions, the average rankings of the other qualities were remarkably close—within an 0.5 range. The neutral quality of leadership was judged most desirable. Next in preference was the ability to get along with others, and then the second neutral quality—technical know-how. The two values of the Protestant ethic were ranked last by the respondents.

In the second grouping (questions 36-40) the executives were asked again to rank the qualities in accordance with their desirability as traits in their associates. One quality characterized a man committed to the Protestant ethic (honesty). Two were reflections of the standards of the organization man (sensitivity to others and dedication to the organization), and two were considered neutral qualities (breadth of interests and judgment). In this grouping the spread was considerably more significant: a full 3.5 points. Honesty ranked as the most valuable quality. The neutral qualities were ranked second and fifth, while the qualities of the organization man were placed in the third and fourth positions.

The third grouping (questions 41-45) asked the respondents to rank qualities as they thought them important for business success. Two of the qualities were those of the organization man (ability to get along with others and dedication to the organization), two were related to the Protestant ethic (honesty and hard work), and one was a neutral factor (family connections and social connections). This last factor was thought to reflect the priority of values suggested by C. Wright Mills as described in a previous chapter. The spread of responses in this group was somewhat less than that of the previous group: 2.19 points. One Protestant-ethic value (hard work) and one organization-man value (ability to get along with others) were clearly preferred, with the former only .06 of a point ahead of the latter. Honesty and dedication to the organization were ranked in third and fourth positions, while the value drawn from The Power Elite was clearly least preferred.

In the fourth grouping (questions 47-52), three alternatives were selected which reflected the values of

Exhibit VI

THE RANKING OF QUALITIES RELATING TO BUSINESS SUCCESS

Quality	Mean Rank	Percent of Respondents Ranking						Total
		1	2	3	4	5	6	
Qualities you would like to find in your associates:								
leadership	2.32	39	22	13	20	6		100
hard work	2.81	15	22	36	22	5		100
ability to get along with others ...	2.50	23	29	28	13	7		100
thrift	4.67	0	0	8	17	75		100
technical know-how	2.71	23	25	17	27	8		100
Qualities you would like to find in your associates:								
sensitivity to others	3.16	10	21	27	28	14		100
honesty	1.94	50	20	17	11	2		100
dedication to the organization ...	3.28	7	19	26	34	14		100
breadth of interests	4.49	3	3	8	15	71		100
judgment	2.16	30	37	21	11	1		100
Qualities important for business success:								
hard work	2.35	32	27	20	15	6		100
family and social connections ...	4.54	6	1	5	10	78		100
ability to get along with others ...	2.41	28	26	23	22	1		100
dedication to the organization ...	3.05	10	19	33	32	6		100
honesty	2.68	23	26	19	23	9		100
Factors influencing ethical conduct in business:								
family training	1.97	58	16	6	11	8	1	100
conduct of superiors	2.82	22	19	28	18	12	1	100
conduct of peers	4.00	1	17	22	19	22	19	100
school and university training	4.51	0	11	11	21	30	27	100
religious training	3.71	9	25	17	9	16	24	100
practices in industry	4.04	10	11	16	22	12	29	100

Which man would you prefer to work with?   Percent of Respondents

an other-directed man*	60
an inner-directed man*	40

*See Appendix A, question 46, for the description of these terms.

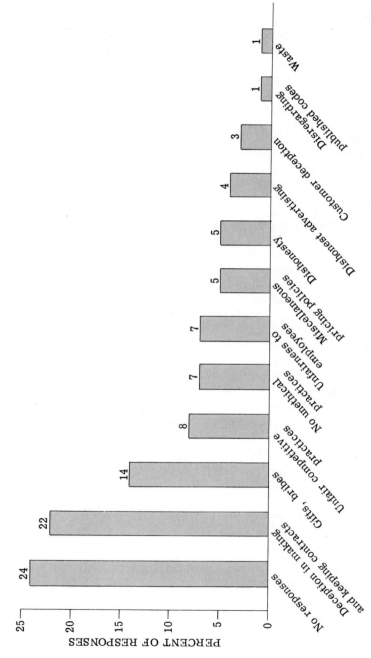

Exhibit VII

"THE ONE PRACTICE I WOULD MOST LIKE TO SEE ELIMINATED"

Riesman's other-directed personality and three which reflected inner-directed values, and the executives were asked to rank these qualities according to their importance in influencing ethical conduct in business. The average ranking of the executives spread over 2.54 positions with no indication of a clear-cut preference for one set of values over the other set. Family training, an inner-directed factor, was judged most influential, while school and university training, another inner-directed factor, was judged least influential. The three other-directed factors, conduct of superiors, conduct of peers, and practices in industry, were rated in second, fourth, and fifth positions; and the remaining inner-directed factor, religious training, was ranked third.

The fifth question in this section presented the respondents with a simple two-point, forced-choice situation. They were asked to show a preference for either an other-directed or an inner-directed type as a business associate. Sixty percent of the respondents preferred the other-directed type, 40 percent the inner-directed associate.

In evaluating the responses to this section of the questionnaire, it must be admitted that the results appear somewhat confused. Perhaps the most reasonable inference which can be drawn is that these executives show no clear-cut or unambiguous preference for either one or the other of the types proposed to them. Rather they show the decided tendency to judge each quality independently of any predetermined pattern. To the extent that this is so, this empirical effort tends to verify the theory of Riesman more than that of Whyte. For Riesman is careful to point out that he is describing certain ideal types and that the majority of men will possess value systems which represent a mixture of both types. Whyte, on the other hand, sees the organization man as more committed to a single set of values than might be indicated by the data of this study.

THE EXECUTIVE SPEAKS OUT: COMMENTS AND OBSERVATIONS

The One Practice Executives Would Most Like To See Eliminated. The third part of the questionnaire consists of a series of

questions which are directed to the discovery of those business practices which the respondents find most objection-
able in the light of their ethical commitments.   Questions
in this section are also directed to uncovering opinion with
respect to ways of improving the ethical climate of American business. Exhibit VII gives a general summary of their
responses.   Seventy-five percent of the respondents took
the time to answer this question, a remarkable indication
of the sincerity and goodwill with which they applied themselves to the questionnaire.   The most frequent practices
mentioned as conflicting with the individual respondent's
ethical standards were related to the making and keeping of
contracts.   This may reflect to some extent the importance
of defense work among the members of the Executive
Training Program, and also among the industries of Southern California in general.   At any rate the following comments of the participants make explicit the nature of their
complaints concerning contract relationships:

- Underbidding and then manipulating the contract to
  regain or reestablish profits.

- Bidding unrealistically low to obtain a contract
  and renegotiating later.

- Knowingly bidding low in order to "buy" a job and
  then hoping to recoup on changes in project.

- Purposeful underbidding with hopes of later price
  increases based on changes in the scope of the
  work.

This sensitivity to the ethical implications of contract bidding may be related to the present competition in this phase
of the aerospace industry. If so, the high priority given to
these practices suggests ethical conduct may deteriorate in
the face of a competitive struggle for survival.

Fourteen percent of the executives thought that the
greatest business lapse in moral conduct was in connection
with the use of bribes and excessive gifts. Obviously this
is an area where it is most difficult to set ironclad bounda-
ries of propriety; yet many of the respondents were troubled by the practices of their companies. As some of them
expressed the practices they would most like to see
eliminated:

- Buyers receiving gifts from suppliers.

- Gratuities to buyers.

- The subtle bribery and compromising of customers as well as the customers' literal demands
for such practices.

- Gifts and expensive entertainment of buyers.

A number of unethical practices were noted by the executives which can best be summed up as methods of unfair
competition. They touch upon the company's relationship
with other companies in the same industry and range from
price discrimination to employee and design pirating.
Pricing practices were notable as among the most frequently objected-to departures from ethical conduct. Some
examples:

- Overpricing.

- Making untrue statements about another company.

- Copying design and pirating technical employees.

- Price cutting and trade discounts.

A full 7 percent of the respondents took exception to
the implication in the question that there were any practices in their industry which were ethically questionable.
Indeed, some of the responses seem to indicate that several executives were annoyed by the suggestion that there
were any such practices in their industries. This annoy-
ance is somewhat reflected in the following responses:

- Maybe I'm lucky to work for such an employer—
but I honestly can't think of any unethical
practices.

- There are none that I can think of that are approved by management.

- None noticed as yet.

- Don't have any.

Several of the responses give indication of ethical
problems which are hard to classify into general categories but nevertheless point to interesting and illuminating
compromises which executives are sometimes forced to

face.   The following responses are illustrative of this situation:

- There is a code of ethics that is supposed to be followed by members of the profession, but in practice many of the items in the Code of Ethics are disregarded.

- In banking much is made of advertising installment interest rates, e. g., 4-1/2 percent auto loans. This rate is the equivalent of 9 percent simple interest.   Some people are confused and think the installment rate is simple interest.   I would like to see all interest rates quoted in simple interest.   Because this is an ethical question, bankers should resolve it themselves rather than wait for legislation.

- Closing their eyes on the part of agents and brokers with their customers in submitting fraudulent claims.

- Pushing stock in small OTC [over-the-counter] securities because the house has a position in them.

Thus the respondents point to a wide area in which business conduct falls short of the ethical ideal.   Nevertheless, one is impressed with the complexity of the dilemmas which some of these practices involve.   Many of them concern judgments which are less than clear-cut, black-and-white decisions.   They are related to a high degree of compromise, and undoubtedly one of their most perplexing aspects is that they are bound up with the very survival of the executive in the business world.   That the executives have spoken so frankly and openly of these moral lapses is encouraging and gives some hope of their interest in remedial measures to bring everyday conduct in closer accord with ethical ideals.

How To Improve Business Ethics. Two questions in this survey were aimed at appraising executive opinion concerning ways of improving the moral atmosphere of business.   In the first of these questions the executives were asked to give their opinions with reference to five suggested steps toward the formation of a more responsible business environment. Exhibit VIII summarizes the executives' opinions of these proposals. Clearly the executives see as the most promising way to improve business ethics the development of some widely accepted general principles. Next in importance for them is the introduction of industry codes of ethical practices. The strong hostility to government regulation as manifested by Exhibit VIII was anticipated, but this student was somewhat taken aback by the decidedly unenthusiastic attitude of executives toward the participation of religious leaders in developing general ethical norms for business. Personal interviews and a number of comments on the questionnaire seem to point to the reason for this attitude toward religious guidance. Many executives believe that the clergy have too little acquaintance with the business environment to appraise with competence the actual problems which these executives face. They express the fear religious leaders will ascribe to such problems a simplicity which belies their actuality.

In the second question dealing with ways of improving the ethical atmosphere in business, the respondents were asked to make suggestions of what they considered effective means of achieving this improvement. Almost 60 percent of the executives took the time to comment on this question; and although their responses are summarized in Exhibit IX, they made many specific suggestions. In discussing the complexity of the moral factor in business decisions, they recognized that business ethics is but a part of the moral standards of the country as a whole. Such awareness was suggested by comments like the following:

- Ethics in business are as personal as ethics in our day-to-day life. Management must preach and practice the highest of ethics if we expect our people to follow. Unethical practices cannot be tolerated at any level. The amount of money involved cannot influence principles.

- Business ethics are not any better or worse than the ethics of individuals in general. Improve the ethics of the individual and place more emphasis on moral rather than material achievement.

- Improve the moral standard of all citizens.

Exhibit VIII

WHAT EXECUTIVES THINK OF PROPOSALS TO IMPROVE BUSINESS ETHICS

Proposal	Percent Approving and Disapproving Each Proposal					
	Approve	Somewhat Approve	No Opinion	Somewhat Disapprove	Disapprove
Develop some widely accepted general principles of business ethics	74	16	5	2	3
Introduce courses in Business Ethics in business schools . .	57	32	5	2	4
Introduce industry codes of ethical practices	62	24	3	5	6
Legislate stronger governmental regulation of business	2	8	3	14	73
Encourage a more active participation of religious leaders in developing general ethical norms for business	13	25	8	19	35

Of frequent mention was the suggestion to publicize the need of ethical conduct in the business milieu. Indeed, it appears that the respondents gave considerable preference to such positive steps toward improvement rather than negative or punitive controls. Among their suggestions were:

- More articles by top men in industry in association trade papers as to the necessity of improving ethical conduct.

- Talk about it. Publish it. Give awards to businessmen with outstanding records of ethical conduct.

- Better disclosure of business practices—publicity.

- Reward successful and ethical people. Commend and publicize ethical practice.

- Introduce ethical conduct as an evaluation criterion in the performance ratings of personnel in sensitive positions.

At the same time the executives were not slow to suggest some penalties and negative incentives to improve business relations, though in many instances they were ambiguous as to what form such penalties should take. Some of their suggestions were:

- Inflict more severe penalties on those who are unethical.

- Publish obvious offenses. Expose dishonesty and punish it accordingly.

- Discharge those who indicate no appreciation for approved ethics.

- More severe penalties for those companies found violating ethical principles—removing them from approved bidders' lists for government contracts, for example.

The executives also see the need to give special attention to the influence of education upon the formation of high ethical ideals. While most saw this education as centering chiefly in the schools, some also noted the importance of family training in the formation of moral character. They

Exhibit IX

HOW TO IMPROVE BUSINESS ETHICS

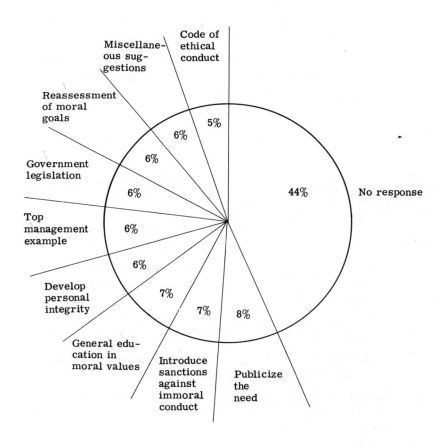

are uncertain as to the precise form such education should take, but they clearly have an awareness of the responsibility of educational institutions in influencing the moral climate of business.   Some of their comments were:

- Start education to make it harder for our society to produce the essentially amoral person.

- Education early in life and continuing through college would gradually accomplish the end result.

- Initial training in ethics during initial schooling starting in grade school. This might be simply done through the medium of civics and social studies classes.

- Better home and family training — (impractical, but the only way I can think of for long-run improvement.)

The respondents also recognize the influence of top management in setting the ethical tone of companies. Without their cooperation, business standards can hardly be improved. With such cooperation, improvement is far more of a possibility.   As several respondents put it:

- By encouraging senior management to become conscious of ethics as a potential problem, the problem will largely solve itself.

- I believe that improvement can be effectively achieved only by the top leaders in a company.

- Leadership in ethical conduct must come right from the top—the president's office.

Some of these respondents felt that the chief executive's major influence would be by way of example. Others felt that the chief executive had to do more. He had to speak frequently about moral integrity and let it be known that this was a quality which was looked for in management selection and promotion.

Another small minority felt that the ethical climate of business was at least in part the responsibility of government, but among these respondents there was a sharp division between those who suggested that more government control was needed and those who recommended a lessening of government regulation. Several singled out the antitrust laws and proposed that a more rigid enforcement of these would do much to improve business ethics. Others cited federal income tax laws and labor legislation as instances of excessive regulation which tended to encourage a deterioration of morality. Several others felt that a general reduction of government control of business would bring about a greater mutual trust both in the relationship of businessmen with each other and in their dealings with the government itself.

Finally, an interesting group of suggestions was related to the establishment of some general ethical norms which could be accepted by the business community as a whole. There was a decided difference of opinion concerning the foundation of such principles, but there seems to be strong support for an effort to develop such general norms. Several participants looked at such a task as a reevaluation of our ethical and moral goals as a nation. Others felt that such guidelines could be established for business without calling for a complete recasting of general ethical values. Some of these comments are worthy of expression here:

- What we need is a moral reevaluation of our goals and attitudes toward our fellowmen. And such a reevaluation need not be religion-based.

- Perhaps the general rule could be applied: Simply consider the consequences of your actions (if unethical) in the light of how you would feel if they were used against you.

- Business ethics can neither be legislated nor codified. But some general principles should be developed which could serve as the cornerstone of some ethical guidelines. Such principles should be based on the Judeo-Christian tradition.

- What we need to do is stir up the mess and start over. Our technology far exceeds our philosophy. There is far too much difference between the top and the bottom. Minority groups have too much influence, e. g. , once started, there is no stopping. Checks and balances are missing. [There is] too much effort placed on politically derived benefits, with no real incentive to do better topwise. Too much social welfare on a dole basis. Give up—I do.

SUMMARY OF THE CHAPTER

This chapter has described the more significant results of the questionnaire in relation to its four parts. Demographic information was first presented to give a composite picture of the executives who made up the test group. They were found to be atypical in the sense that they seemed more educated and more successful than the average executive of a similar age. Their ethical standards were explored as they were related to the 26 cases which comprised the first part of the questionnaire. Their responses point to the fact that they have no clear-cut or universal ethical code which can easily be applied to all members of the group. Instead they are a group of men with complex and sometimes even conflicting values but, nevertheless, are vitally concerned with the moral dimensions of their business decisions. While firmly committed to the profit motive as the legitimate objective of private enterprise, they are almost universal in recognizing that business decisions need to take into account certain social responsibilities.

In responding to the second part of the questionnaire (the ranking questions) these executives show no unambiguous predilection towards the values of the organization man or the other-directed man over the values of the Protestant ethic or the inner-directed man. On the contrary, they tend to judge the relevance of certain values in an independent manner rather than according to any predetermined pattern. In their judgment some virtues of the Protestant ethic remain of importance (industry, honesty), while certain others seem of less relevance to modern business conditions (thrift). They express an appreciation for the values of the organization man and the other-directed man but show no unequivocal pattern of preferring such values above all others. In general, they seem to be a group of men with complex and conflicting values which defy any single classification into neat value systems.

In the third part of the questionnaire the executives were given opportunity to express their opinions at length with reference to the ethical problems they faced in business and the means they felt most effective for the improvement of business ethics.   Again the executives reveal a wide variety of opinions in both these areas and consistently reveal the pattern of independent judgment which was noted above.

Chapter 6

RESULTS OF THE QUESTIONNAIRE: PART II

INTRODUCTION

THE PURPOSE OF THIS CHAPTER

The objective of this chapter is to interpret data of the questionnaire in the light of the several scales which have been explained in Chapter 5. Thus it does not have reference to an independent part of the questionnaire, but rather is a particular interpretation of certain cases which appear in the questionnaire's first part. These cases were chosen for the scales both on the basis of the opinion of five impartial judges and also on the basis of a careful analysis of their degree of significance as measured by Chi-square tabulations in the pretest group. The cases constituting the scales were selected from the total number of cases in the questionnaire. The present chapter, then, offers an analysis of some of the case material contained in the previous chapter, but here such information is considered as it bears on the specific norms embodied in the two scales.

The previous chapter analyzed the data of the questionnaire from a collective viewpoint. Major attention was given to group attitudes and opinions, and no effort was made to appraise individual performance. The present chapter is directed to the analysis of some of this same information from the individual viewpoint. What is asked here is whether or not the questionnaire can give us any new insights with reference to the individual codes of the respondents. Can the questionnaire be used to give a picture of the scope of the individual's ethical standards, and can these standards be compared with one another in any way?

The theoretical implications and limitations of this analysis have been explained in a previous chapter and need to be kept in mind during the subsequent discussion. Indeed, one motive for treating this material in a separate chapter is the desire to keep the tentative nature of these data carefully distinguished from the previous analysis. Several problems are peculiar to the interpretation of the questionnaire in terms of scales; and by a separate presentation of this aspect of the study, care can be given to the consideration of these problems.

THE OBJECTIVES OF THE SCALES

As has been explained in a previous chapter, the scales have not been designed to rate an executive against some commonly accepted standard of business ethics.   Rather, they attempt to assay the dimensions of the respondent's ethical commitments.   The cases were constructed with a view to embracing as many different kinds of value decisions as were feasible.   It may well be that an executive who is ethical to a very high degree may consider certain of the cases as not pertaining to his ethical code.   Such might lead to a low score for this participant on one or both of the scales.   What such a low score means is simply that the respondent under consideration has a limited range of ethical commitments relative to other executives; and that does not necessarily imply a propensity towards dishonesty, lack of integrity, or other moral deficiency.

Thus these scales should be considered more as indicators than as strict indices.   Indices of various types, like the cost-of-living index, measure accurately and objectively very minute changes in empirical phenomena.   Indicators, on the other hand, like the various economic indicators, are far less exact and primarily signal the direction of changes in empirical phenomena.   It is suggested that the following scales be viewed more as indicators than as indices.   While it is believed that they do reveal some significant information about the ethical standards of the respondents, and while the "scores" of the two scales are expressed with mathematical exactitude, it is not proposed that these scales be interpreted as revealing a precise and exact statistical measurement of ethical commitment.

METHOD OF SCORING THE SCALES

The method of scoring the scales was quite simple. Each case involved a range of choices between personal gain and support of some social or ethical value. The responses to the questions were scored one through five, as the response ranged from the choice of personal gain through the choice of total support of the social value. The scores of each of the cases involved in the particular scale were added together to give a total score for the scale. The range and meaning of these scores will be discussed more in detail with respect to each of the two scales.

THE BUSINESS-ETHICS SCALE

THE SCORE RANGE AND ITS MEANING

The 11 cases which comprise the business-ethics scale were identified in Chapter 4; and there the meaning and significance of this scale were explained in detail, together with the criteria which are the objective standards of this scale. The lowest possible score for this scale is 11, a scoring of one for each of the cases involved. Any score between 11 and 33 indicates that the respondent has, on an average, given a kind of weighted preference to the direction of personal gain over the direction of support of social values. This preference is considered weighted inasmuch as it gives more significance to a firm response than to one revealing a degree of doubt or hesitancy. At the score of 33, the respondent can be considered as balanced between personal gain and the support of social values, for this score represents a weighted average opinion of "unable to decide." For purposes of identity this score will be called the neutral position on the scale. From 34 to 55, the score shows an increasing preference for the support of social values at the sacrifice of personal gain. The highest possible score of 55 indicates that the respondent in every case chose social values over his own personal gain, and this with no hesitation or doubt.

THE PERFORMANCE

How did the executives score on the cases which comprise the personal-ethics scale? Exhibit X gives a picture

of their scores, and Exhibits XI and XII portray this information in graphic form.   Only 5 percent of the respondents
registered a weighted average which indicated an overall
choice of personal gain over social values, and in each of
these cases the score indicated only a slight leaning toward
personal gain.   One respondent scored 33, the neutral position on the scale; and a full 94 percent of the respondents
showed a weighted preference for support of social values.
The median score was 43, which indicated an average response at about the half-way point up the ethical side of the
scale.   Only one respondent went down the line to choose
unequivocally support of social values in every instance,
but a full 4 percent of the respondents did so in all but a
single instance.

INTERPRETATION OF THE SCORES

On the whole, the executives seem to score rather high
on the personal-ethics scale.   Indeed, there is indication
that the scale does not adequately measure the "ceilings"
of the personal-ethics commitment of at least some of the
respondents.   Exhibit XI gives evidence of this in that the
curve is skewed well to the right of a normal curve.   It is
believed that this skewness does more than point to the
limitations of the questionnaire.   It also seems to point to
the relatively high ethical standards of the executives
themselves.   Fundamentally, executives seem committed
to values of the ethical order.   When faced with the
decisions which are commonly judged to have ethical implications, the respondents show an appreciation of the noneconomic and social values at stake.

In another respect, however, the results present a less
optimistic picture.   In the previous chapter it was indicated
that in the answers to the individual cases, the participants
manifested a wide divergence of opinions.   In comparing
the individual scales of the respondents, this same fact
comes to the fore in a new light.   Not only are there differences of opinion in regard to individual cases, but, more
seriously, there is a difference in the range of components
in the standards of different individuals.   Some individuals
answered this section of the questionnaire in such a way as
to suggest that they regard all the cases as having ethical
implications.   Others seem to think that the number of

Exhibit X

THE PERSONAL-ETHICS SCALE

Total Score	Number of Respondents	Cumulative Number of Respondents
11	0	0
12	0	0
13	0	0
14	0	0
15	0	0
16	0	0
17	0	0
18	0	0
19	0	0
20	0	0
21	0	0
22	0	0
23	0	0
24	0	0
25	0	0
26	0	0
27	1	1
28	1	2
29	1	3
30	0	3
31	1	4
32	1	5
33	1	6
34	1	7
35	4	11
36	1	12
37	5	17
38	2	19
39	5	24
40	8	32
41	5	37
42	10	47
43	8	55
44	7	62
45	4	66
46	5	71
47	4	75
48	8	83
49	3	86
50	1	87
51	7	94
52	4	98
53	0	98
54	4	102
55	1	103

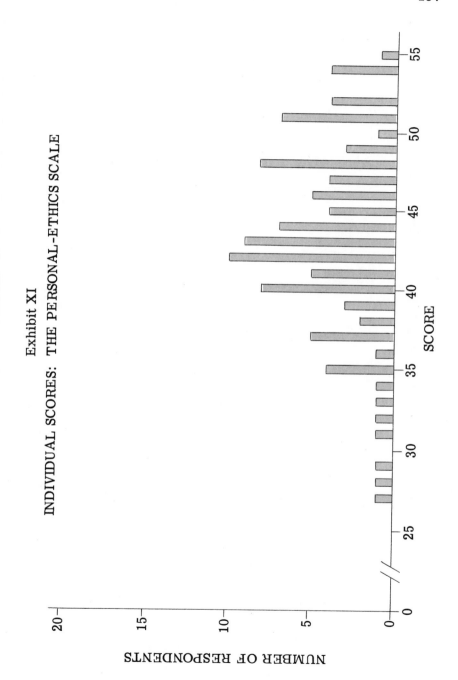

Exhibit XI

INDIVIDUAL SCORES: THE PERSONAL-ETHICS SCALE

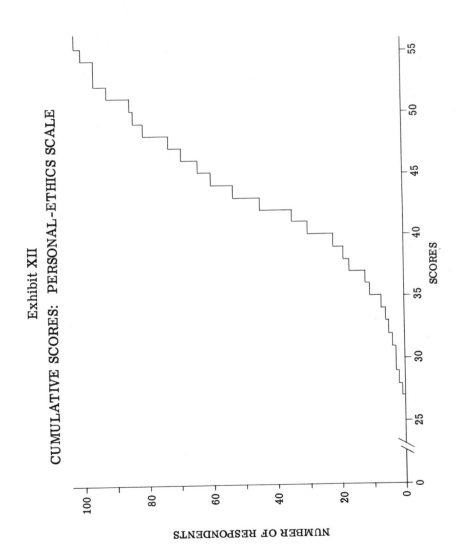

Exhibit XII

CUMULATIVE SCORES: PERSONAL-ETHICS SCALE

cases with real ethical problems are few. Thus the questionnaire reveals not only the presence of different prudential judgments which are based on different ethical ideals, but, even more seriously, it also reveals that the executives differ considerably among themselves in their judgment of the extent to which ethical standards have a bearing on common business practices. This matter will be returned to in the next chapter.

THE SOCIAL-RESPONSIBILITY SCALE

THE SCORING RANGE AND ITS MEANING

The social-responsibility scale has been discussed with some detail in Chapter 5. There the meaning of social responsibility as understood in this scale was considered, and criteria were established to identify commitments to these values in the concrete order. Here it is necessary to relate these criteria to the actual score tabulation which was used.

Since there are just seven cases in this scale, the lowest possible score for the scale is 7, which represents a score of one for each of the cases involved. Such a score is to be interpreted as meaning that in every single instance the respondent chose without qualification personal gain to the support of the social values relating to this scale. Any score between 7 and 21 indicates that the respondent has on an average given a weighted preference to the direction of personal gain over the direction of support of social values. The meaning of this weighted score has been explained in the previous section. At the score of 21, the respondent can be considered as balanced between personal gain and support of the related social values, for this score represents the neutral position described earlier. As the score rises from 22 to the scale maximum of 35, the respondent indicates an increasing preference for the support of the related social values over personal gain. And the maximum score of 35 indicates that the respondent in every case chose support of the related social value over personal gain without perceiving any need to qualify his opinion.

THE PERFORMANCE

Scores on the social responsibility scale show some significant variations from the scores of the business ethics scale. Exhibits XIII, XIV, and XV summarize the information relevant to the social-responsibility scale. Almost immediately noticeable in Exhibit XIV is the fact that the distribution curve of the scores approaches a more normal curve than in the former scale. The median score is found at 21, which marks the neutral position on the scale and represents a balance between commitment to personal gain and commitment to support of social values. The spread of the scores is also considerably broader in this scale than in the business ethics scale, though there is still a marked skewness of the distribution curve to the right. The lowest score of ten approximates a rather complete rejection of the values of social responsibility, while the highest score of 33 shows an almost complete acceptance of them at the cost of personal gain. Approximately 90 percent of the respondents score less than 26 on the scale, a position comparable to the median score on the business ethics scale.

INTERPRETATION OF THE SCORES

The executives seem notably less willing to accept the values of the social-responsibility scale than those of the business-ethics scale. A full 50 percent of the respondents can be considered as having a negative attitude toward these values, at least as they are presented in the particular cases comprising the scale. This is believed to be significant, especially when compared with the high scores of the business-ethics scale. These executives show a greater reluctance to sacrifice personal gain for social goals than they do for the well-recognized principles of honesty and integrity. This does not necessarily imply an irresponsibility on their part. Rather it may simply point to the fact that they are inclined to agree with Henry Ford II when he said, "The worst sin I can commit as a businessman is to fail to seek maximum long-term profitability by all decent and lawful means. To do so is to subvert

Exhibit XIII

THE SOCIAL-RESPONSIBILITY SCALE

Total Score	Number of Respondents	Cumulative Number of Respondents
7	0	0
8	0	0
9	0	0
10	1	1
11	1	2
12	0	2
13	0	2
14	2	4
15	6	10
16	5	15
17	3	18
18	12	30
19	11	41
20	7	48
21	11	59
22	6	65
23	10	75
24	6	81
25	5	86
26	6	92
27	3	95
28	1	96
29	1	97
30	2	99
31	2	101
32	1	102
33	1	103
34	0	103
35	0	103

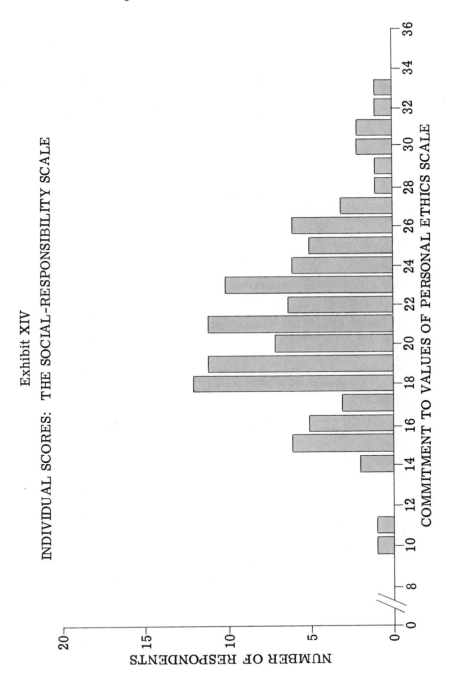

Exhibit XIV

INDIVIDUAL SCORES: THE SOCIAL-RESPONSIBILITY SCALE

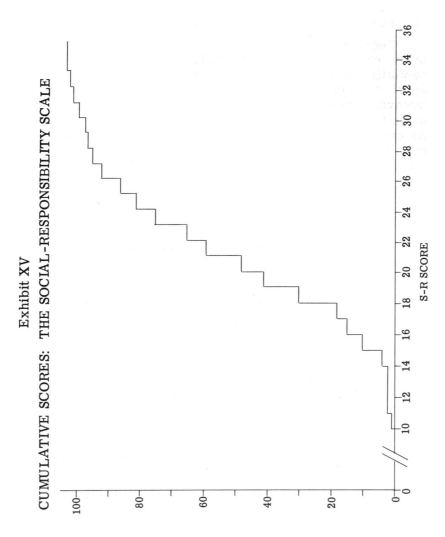

Exhibit XV

CUMULATIVE SCORES: THE SOCIAL-RESPONSIBILITY SCALE

economic reason. "[1] Many of our executives seem to agree with this position, which sees the businessman as best serving community interests by devoting himself to performing his economic function in the most efficient way possible.

There is reason to believe that the social-responsibility scale has more effectively tested the "ceilings" of commitment than did the previous scale, though in this respect, too, more could be desired. The distribution curve, however, more clearly approaches the normal curve; and while the extremes are relatively short, they nevertheless do exhibit a gradual tapering off of scores. This may permit somewhat more confidence in appraising the commitments of executives in the area of social responsibility. The business-ethics scale seems more reliable in the area of revealing the minimum commitments of the respondents. The social-responsibility scale probably more effectively tests the full range of commitments.

The scores of this scale point to a wider divergence of opinion with regard to the values of social responsibility than was found in the section dealing with the business-ethics values. As in the case of the business-ethics values, this divergence points not only to a difference of opinion concerning whether a particular case is relevant to the individual's standards, but more fundamentally to the range of values which need to be respected in this area. This range goes from the recognition of practically no unambiguous values in the area to a nearly full commitment to all the values contained in the cases. Such a result highlights the conclusions of other studies that there is a wide divergence in ethical standards and gives some indication that this divergence is found both in the dimension of what is and what is not a value which should take precedence over personal gain, and also in the dimension of how many various values are related to the individual's standard.

---

[1] Henry Ford II, "What America Expects of Industry," an address delivered at the Annual Meeting of the Michigan State Chamber of Commerce, Detroit, Michigan, October 2, 1962. Published as a pamphlet by the Public Relations Division of the Ford Motor Company, Dearborn, Michigan.

THE RELATIONSHIP BETWEEN THE SCALES

THE PROBLEM

What is the relationship between the two scales? Do those executives who score high on one scale tend to score high on the other also? Certain theoretical inferences might lead one to suspect that such is not the case. As explained earlier, the scales in this paper draw somewhat on the concepts of Richard Eells, who posed two ideal types of ethical creeds for corporations. The business-ethics scale and the social-responsibility scale of this present effort are roughly modeled on the ideal types described by Eells. It is Eells' contention that corporations tend to one or the other of these models; and based on his analysis, an early hypothesis in the present study proposed the same kind of dichotomy between the two scales as they apply to individuals. It was believed that most of the executives would prove to be highly ethical but that the expression of their ethical commitments would be sharply divided into those which were limited to the parameters of the business-ethics scale and those which went beyond to include those of the social-responsibility scale.

THE DATA

Exhibit XVI presents a scattergram which attempts to assess the validity of this hypothesis. If the hypothesis is to be verified, there should be heavy concentration of scores in the lower and upper parts of the right end of the scattergram. Such clusters of scores did not appear; and, quite contrary to expectations, another pattern, which must be interpreted in a different manner, is in evidence. The scattergram reveals a noticeable, though not a striking, pattern for the scores to rise on the vertical axis as they become higher on the horizontal axis. The scattergram was divided into quadrants and the pattern tested for significance by means of the Chi-square test. The pattern has a .03 level of significance and thus tends to offer evidence that the hypothesis explained above is positively excluded as far as this particular group of respondents is concerned.

The evidence does seem to point to the fact that as individuals score higher on the business-ethics scale they

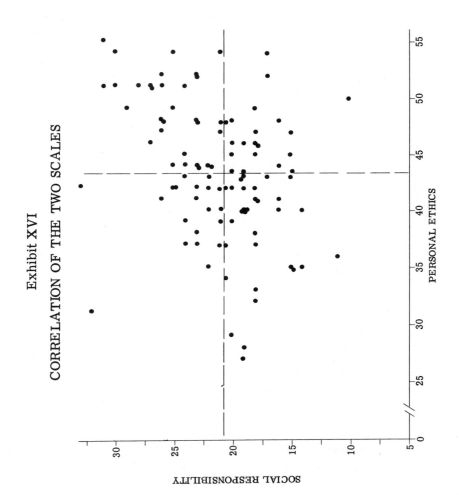

Exhibit XVI

CORRELATION OF THE TWO SCALES

also tend to score higher on the social-responsibility scale. Thus there seems to be reason for asserting a positive relationship between the individual's commitment to the values of each of the scales. As the individual's commitment to one of the scales rises, so does his commitment to the other scale; and as his commitment to one or another of the scales decreases, so does his commitment to the other scale. Thus social responsibility, as it has been embodied in the cases in this study, appears not as something independent of one's personal ethical commitment, but seems to be intimately bound up with one's total ethical standard.

SUMMARY OF THE CHAPTER

This chapter has attempted to analyze the data of the questionnaire with reference to two scales which were explained in detail in Chapter 4. The previous chapter analyzed data in terms of group characteristics. This present chapter uses some of the case data to evaluate the individual's ethical commitment. The point was made that while numerical scores would be used throughout the analysis, no mathematical exactness was being proposed as a precise measurement of an individual respondent's value system. Rather what was aimed at was a concise and greatly simplified picture of the respondent's attitude toward ethical and social values.

With respect to the business-ethics scale, two salient facts seem to stand out. First, the executives scored very high on this test. The respondents manifest a sincere concern for and interest in questions involving honesty, observance of the law, and personal integrity. In these areas they had fewer unequivocal responses than in subsequent sections of the questionnaire, and this would seem to point to a basic and fundamental orientation to ethical values. Secondly, the executives manifest a wide difference of opinion as to the relevance of some particular cases to their ethical standards and also as to the range of components which go into their total ethical value systems.

With respect to the social-responsibility scale, there are also two points of particular note. First, the respondents show considerably more hesitation to sacrifice personal gain for the values of this scale than for the values of the previous scale. They also gave more reserved or qualified responses to cases relating to these scales than to the previous scale. Almost 50 percent of the respondents on the average preferred personal gain to the support of the values of this scale, and only 10 percent averaged higher than a "somewhat approve" response to the support of the social values. Secondly, there is reason to believe that this scale has more effectively measured the ceilings of commitment than did the first scale and thus manifests a reservation for the values of social responsibility.

Finally, an analysis of the relationship between the two scales fails to substantiate an earlier belief that respondents would tend to rank high on either one of the scales, but not on both. Rather, it was discovered that there was a marked tendency for those who scored high on one scale to do the same on the other.

Chapter 7

A TENTATIVE STATEMENT OF ETHICAL GUIDES

INTRODUCTION

This chapter is designed to present by way of conclusion to the present study a tentative statement of ethical guides. It is hoped that this statement will contribute to the existing literature of business ethics by suggesting some commonly accepted theoretical norms which are suitable as the basis of an ethical evaluation of specific business practices.

In the attempt to develop theoretical guides for business decisions, the present chapter is only partially dependent on the previous sections of this study. While both the investigation of historical influences and the empirical data of the study have contributed to the content of the guides, a number of other studies have also been considered. The guides by no means resolve the ethical complexities of many business situations. They are simply suggested as a formulation of widely held ethical postulates in the business community. Together they do not make a code of ethics with ready-made solutions to specific business problems, but rather serve as a formulation of ethical principles which are generally accepted in the business community and which can serve as the basis of a detailed discussion of specific problems of business ethics.

DESCRIPTION OF THE TENTATIVE STATEMENT

A GENERAL DESCRIPTION

This formulation consists of the organization of ethical guides on two levels of understanding. The first level includes a series of primary guides which are most basic and theoretical. These primary guides may be looked upon as the foundation of the ethical theory and correspond roughly to the objective level of the function of planning.[1] The second level of guides, the middle guides, as they will be called, are somewhat more directed to concrete problems, but are still quite broad in their content and are concerned more with the formation of ethical thinking than with the direct problems of ethical conduct. These middle guides correspond to the policy level of planning.

THE TENTATIVE STATEMENT AS A MODEL

Exhibit XVII illustrates the relationship of these two levels of guides to the concrete decision-making process. Primary guides are seen as underlying the individual's ethical code and as the foundation of the code itself. These guides are most general in nature and probably are the most widely accepted of the guides. The middle guides are norms which are established as means of achieving the ethical goals expressed by the primary guides. These norms, like the primary guides, are general in nature and are directed to helping the executive in the formation of his attitudes or his thinking toward the ethical dimensions of

Exhibit XVII

THE STRUCTURE OF AN ETHICAL DECISION

Ethical Decision

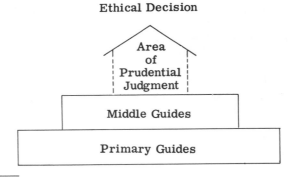

---

[1]Harold Koontz and Cyril O'Donnell, Principles of Management (New York: McGraw-Hill Book Co. , 1964), pp. 74-75.

business decisions. Nevertheless, they are more specific than the primary guides and represent a bridge between the goals of business as a social institution and the activity of the individual businessman. They attempt to express the values of the primary guides as they have bearing on the individual executive. Thus the step from the primary to the middle guides, while remaining on the theoretical level, represents a transfer from the goals of society to the norms for individual ethical thinking. The middle guides are meant to assure that the action and decisions of the individual are in accord with the broader goals of business as a social institution.

Exhibit XVII also reveals an area between the guides and the ethical decision based upon these guides. This "area of prudential judgment" is an attempt to illustrate the gap which exists between abstract norms and concrete situations which businessmen face. Several factors contribute to the existence of this gap. First, circumstances surrounding decisions are constantly changing, and these circumstances demand consideration by executives. Circumstances may be so important that they vitally affect the ethical direction of the decision. Further, it is possible that in some business decisions two ethical guides may be in conflict, one supporting each alternative of any given decision. This is an area that cannot be charted perfectly by theory. Rather, it represents the point where individual judgment needs to weigh and balance the relevancy of theory to the specific situation.

This area of prudential judgment illustrates an important point with regard to this model. It is not proposed—indeed, it would be foolish to propose—that guides or principles can supply automatic or mechanical solutions to ethical problems so that, given any particular ethical problem, some particular guide will remove all doubt about the ethical direction of a given decision.[2] This type of model may have its place in the physical or engineering sciences, but not here. Rather, the present model illustrates that ethical guides somewhat resemble the backlog of knowledge which a surgeon brings to the operating table. Such

---

[2] This point has been discussed at length by William C. Frederick, "The Growing Concern Over Business Responsibility," California Management Review, II: 4, Summer, 1960; cf. especially p. 61.

knowledge is of considerable value, and yet it must be applied with attention to the unique and specific circumstances of each case.

If the following exploratory effort toward the formulation of ethical guides be viewed in this light, its true usefulness becomes apparent. It is not a system for removing the judgment or the evaluative process from the decisions of the businessman. Rather it is an aid, another instrument at hand to make his decision more likely to conform with his own and with society's ethical ideals.

THE PRIMARY GUIDES

The primary guides of business are probably few in number, but they are undoubtedly the most important influences on the ethical character of business conduct. They are very broad in content, and at the same time they are remote from the immediate decision-making process. But for all that, they are still a most important influence on business ethics. They lie at the roots of the American value system, for they are to a great extent widely accepted and are almost self-evident. In this sense they may be regarded as similar to mathematical axioms. Nevertheless, any logical framework of ethical norms will need to begin with these basic and pervasive guides.

These guides are capable of formulation in several modes. In the present expression of ethical guides, the primary norms will be described in three formulas.

THE GUIDE OF SOCIAL INSTITUTIONS

Ethical action is based upon the support of the social institutions which are generally accepted by a given society.

Meaning of the Guide. Alfred North Whitehead has observed that "a sense of responsibility for the continuance of a social system is basic to any morality."[3] This truth is so fundamental that it is placed at the beginning of the present synthesis. In a certain sense it forms the basis of all the

---

[3]Quoted in Chester I. Barnard, "Elementary Conditions of Business Morals," California Management Review, I(1): 3, Fall, 1959.

guides to follow, for to a certain degree the other guides are developed from this basic value.

The term "social institutions" is itself somewhat ambiguous. Hobhouse has observed that "The term is so variously used that it is doubtful if it has a single root meaning common to all its applications."[4] In the sense that it is used in this first guide, the meaning is rather broad. C. A. Ellwood has given expression to the meaning of institutions as used in this first guide. As he describes them, "Institutions may be defined as habitual ways of living together which have been sanctioned, systematized, and established by the authority of communities."[5] In this sense, institutions are the outgrowth of social habits established by groups. Usually they have stronger sanctions attached to them than do customs.

The first guide expresses the need of the ethical man to support the social institutions which have been established in the society of which he is a part. Fundamentally the need for such support is rooted in the very purpose of human society. Chester Barnard, in his penetrating analysis of formal organizations, has expressed the primary purpose of such organizations as the attempt to overcome the biological limitation of man by means of cooperation.[6] In a very effective way, social institutions, especially when supported by ethical guides, make cooperation possible by providing a relatively stable environment in which human cooperation can take place. It establishes, by common agreement, an area in which an individual can reasonably predict the response of others to his actions, and thus it makes possible cooperative effort with some degree of certainty and stability.

It is especially the relation of social institutions to values that makes them the subject of this first guide. Social institutions are in reality an embodiment and concrete expression of the values which a particular civilization has come to accept. The individual who recognizes

---

[4] L. T. Hobhouse, Social Development (London: Allen and Unwin. 1924), p. 48.

[5] C. A. Ellwood, Psychology of Human Society (New York: D. Appleton and Company, 1925), pp. 90-91.

[6] Chester I. Barnard, The Functions of the Executive (Cambridge: Harvard University Press, 1938), p. 26.

that his own private action needs to support the commonly accepted social institutions of his culture is in fact acknowledging the need to contribute to the cooperation which is the basic purpose of human society.   Accepted social institutions are a mirror of a society's functioning ethics.   There are, of course, conventionally taboo social institutions which serve criminals and similar underground groups, which do not set the tone of society as a whole. Thus social institutions, as understood in this guide, are limited to those which are commonly accepted.   Fundamentally, then, this first guide expresses the need for individual human action to be related to the objectives and the goals of society itself.

Support of the Guide in the Present Study.   As has been observed, the guides have not been derived exclusively from the research embodied in the present study.   Rather, they draw upon a number of studies concerned with business ethics. Nevertheless, since the guides do represent important hypotheses for contemporary business society, support of these guides should be evidenced in the previous sections of the present study.

The guide of social institutions can find support in both the historical and empirical sections of the present study. The religious values of all three major faiths manifest a deep respect for the social institutions of man.   The Protestant ethic itself directly reflects values which are associated more with an individual rather than with social orientation.   Yet it is clear that a responsible support of existing social institutions is implicitly contained in its value hierarchy.   Early Puritan communities in Colonial America reflect the concern of the early settlers for civil harmony.   It would be difficult to understand such concern apart from the values of the Protestant ethic of which it is a natural part. Jewish religious values even more explicitly support this guide, as it is, indeed, a corollary of the Jewish religious value of social consciousness.   The guide is also closely related to the Catholic emphasis on the social nature of man.

Empirical support of this guide can also be found in the present study. Executive responses to the questionnaire reflected a high degree of personal responsibility for social order.   The electrical-equipment price-fixing case (A) and the case dealing with a political bribe (S), discussed in Chapter 6, manifest a strong willingness to sacrifice personal gain to support widely accepted social institutions. Other cases less directly reflect this same viewpoint (e. g., F and E). Thus, empirically, executives show an inclination to embrace values which reflect this guide.

Application of the Guide. The guide has special significance for the businessman, for the business system itself is a social institution, and as such is a part of another, larger social system. Responsibility for the vitality of the macro-system is fundamental to the existence of civilization itself and to the security of all members of society. The businessman, then, needs to act in such a way that his decisions contribute to the welfare of the social system, or at least do the social system no overall harm. This is the condition of his living in society and of his sharing in the fruits of cooperative effort. If at times this norm demands of the individual businessman substantial sacrifices, these must be regarded as the "cost" of living in society.

In its general expression this guide probably enjoys wide, if not universal, acceptance by the business community. As it is developed more explicitly and applied to the area of middle guides, it touches on areas of controversy. But even in its general expression, it has rather far-reaching implications for the businessman.

First of all, this guide expresses the public nature of every business. It is by reason of this orientation to the public good that business itself receives its raison d'etre and the legitimacy of the power which it exercises. Fundamentally, the existence of the American institution of business is dependent upon public acceptance of its usefulness to personal, national, and social goals of the American people as a whole. The basis of this acceptance is the conviction on the part of the American people that business serves or contributes to this common welfare. Hence this guide lies at the very roots of the business system itself. And the recognition of its existence by businessmen is of the greatest importance for the survival of the business system.

In another respect this norm is of great importance because it is the basis of the modern discussion concerning

the social responsibilities of the businessman. Fundamentally, such responsibility lies in the recognition by the
businessman of his commitment to other values of the
American people which are outside the business system.
Thus if the business system is not closed, but rather one
which is influenced by and influences other social systems,
then the businessman, in order to understand properly his
role in society and his relationship with other segments of
society, needs to recognize the validity of this guide and
to condition his activities to the reality which it expresses.

THE GUIDE OF RESPECT FOR OTHERS

A proper support of social institutions includes a
recognition of the rights and the obligations of others.

Meaning of the Guide. Just as the first primary guide laid
the basis for the businessman's need to view his function
with respect to social institutions, the present guide has its
objective to provide a basic norm for the businessman's
relationship with other individuals. Social institutions are
built upon interpersonal relationships. In the cooperative
effort that is implied in any organization, the harmonious
relationships among individuals are fundamental to the
achievement of organizational objectives. Thus there is
need to establish a general guide relevant to interpersonal
relations both within and without the firm in a comprehensive synthesis of ethical norms. This second guide is
directed to this need.

A word of clarification is needed in regard to the use
of the word "obligation." If it is basic to the support of
social institutions that an individual respect the rights of
others, it is equally fundamental to understand the mutuality
of this relationship. Indeed, it is impossible for one to act
in recognition of the rights of others unless he can reasonably surmise that others will treat him in a like manner.
Upon such an assumption are the interpersonal relationships of society based. Human cooperation would be
impossible if individuals could not reasonably expect others
to recognize one another's rights. Thus in a real sense
the very acceptance of membership in society implies a

certain obligation to respect the rights of others. And this is the obligation which is referred to in this second guide.[7]

Support of the Guide in the Present Study.   Little needs to be said about the support of this guide in the research sections of this study.   Certainly the presence of values embodied in this guide were patently manifest in both the historical and empirical phases of the research.   The guide is so basic to the values of the Protestant ethic that it can almost be identified as a postulate of this religious creed.   It is less evident in Jewish religious values,[8] though certainly respect for the individual is an integral part of the value of attachment to life described in Chapter 2.   Catholic thought expresses this value in the concept of the dignity of the individual. In the empirical research, executives frequently manifested an appreciation of the rights and obligations of other individuals (Cases T, W, G, K, X, and V).

Applications to Business.   The guide of respect for others is fundamental to a wide variety of business activities which are related to ethical values.   All those activities which imply a quid pro quo relationship and are concerned with questions of justice are rooted in this primary norm.   Thus the simple honesty which is implied in a business exchange, the payment of debts, fidelity to commitments, truthfulness in communications—all these and many other business activities are founded on the conviction that businessmen will recognize in others a basic human dignity which lies at the roots of the rights and privileges of others. This in turn puts responsibility on the shoulders of the businessman.

It is interesting to note that the vast majority of businessmen give public support to this guide.   Businessmen are quick to explain how their own dealings do not infringe upon or abuse the rights of others.   Business history contains some remarkable examples of the extremes some executives will go to in order to show that their dealings

---

[7]C. H. Waddington has developed the idea of ethics as functionally related to man's effort to live in social relations with other men. Cf. his The Ethical Animal (London: George Allen & Unwin, Ltd., 1960), especially pp. 60-61.

[8]Alfred Kutzik in Social Work and Jewish Values (Washington, D. C.: Public Affairs Press, 1959), pp. 13, 24; quoted on p. 35 of the present work.

have not been unjust. [9] This ritual of defending one's action as just is religiously practiced precisely because business-men do recognize the indispensable requirement that indi-viduals recognize the rights of others in modern industrial society. [10] Undoubtedly, this practice can be traced to the almost universal recognition of justice as a traditional value in Western civilization.

THE GUIDE OF INDIVIDUAL INTEGRITY

A proper support of social institutions supposes a personal commitment to individual integrity.

Meaning Of The Guide. This third primary guide is directed to the relationship of the support of social institutions to individual integrity. Integrity as used in this study has reference to a certain moral unity or wholeness in the character of individuals. This wholeness is expressed by a consistency between the moral standards and ideals of the individual and his conduct. In this sense, a person who possesses such integrity directs his conduct in accordance with the ethical standards which he has accepted on an intellectual or theoretical level. Frequently, he is regarded by his acquaintances as a "man of principle" because he makes a sincere effort to apply known ethical standards to his everyday activity.

This norm is also axiomatic in character and is widely accepted in our culture without the need for a strictly scientific proof of its validity. In this respect it is proba-bly an immediate corollary of Western man's appreciation of the dignity of the individual. Regardless of one's belief concerning the nature of man, Western civilization has traditionally recognized the individual as something more than a sophisticated complex of electrons, and this high

---

[9]Typical of this attitude was the observation of a General Elec-tric executive involved in the 1961 electrical-equipment price-fixing scandal: "Sure, collusion was illegal, but it wasn't unethical." From Richard Austin Smith, "The Incredible Electrical Conspiracy," Fortune, LXIII(4): 135, April, 1961.

[10]Bernard W. Dempsey, S. J., "The Roots of Business Respon-sibility," Harvard Business Review, XXVII(4): 395, July, 1949.

esteem of the individual is in no small part based on the moral responsibility implied in this guide of personal integrity.

Indeed, acceptance of this guide of individual integrity can be regarded as the recognition of personal responsibility for one's own conduct, and such recognition is fundamental to the very possibility of an ethical theory. For unless businessmen perceive the presence of an obligation, a moral responsibility to avoid what they themselves consider unethical, ethical standards will have no practical meaning.

Support of the Guide in Present Research. The present guide can be observed as operational in both the religious and the personal value systems explored in the previous sections of this study. Integrity plays a basic role in the ethical content of almost all religions, and evidence of its esteemed position in the three major religious faiths is ample. In the limited discussion of religious values of Chapters 1, 2, and 3, no explicit treatment of integrity was included because attention was given to less obvious aspects of these religious creeds. However, evidence of the Protestant, Jewish, and Catholic acceptance of the value embodied in this guide hardly requires testimonial support in a study of the present character. The conclusions of other scholars [11] can be readily accepted in the interest of devoting full attention to other aspects of the ethical content of religious creeds.

A number of cases in the empirical phase of the present study support the conclusion that the guide of integrity is operational in the personal value systems of the majority of the respondents. In a sense, every case reflects the influence of this value, for executive approval or disapproval implies a belief that a man's conduct should be consistent with his moral beliefs. But the guide is particularly

---

[11]For a development of this point by a Protestant scholar, see: Wesley H. Hager, "Ethics in Business in the Judeo-Christian Tradition." For a similar treatment by a Jewish scholar, see Philip S. Gershon, "The Jewish Approach to Business Ethics." A Catholic expression of this value is found in Thomas F. Divine, S. J., "The Catholic Tradition in Economic and Business Ethics." All these essays are found in Joseph W. Towle, (ed.) Ethics and Standards in American Business (Boston: Houghton-Mifflin Company, 1964).

operative in Cases S (campaign contribution for a construction contract) and K (recommending inferior bonds).
In each of these cases the respondents were asked their
evaluation of a situation in which profit maximization was
chosen at the sacrifice of personal moral convictions. In
each of these cases the respondents were in relative agreement in their disapproval of such activity, thus revealing
support of this guide.

Applications to Business. This is a truth that has been recognized by the business community on both a practical and
a theoretical level. Francis X. Sutton relates individual
integrity to the concept of individualism, which is a re-
curring theme in business creeds:

> Individualism has two main aspects, an injunc-
> tion of responsibility and an affirmation of freedom.
> First, it involves individual moral responsibility in
> the sense that each individual must direct his actions
> according to moral norms and be prepared to accept
> the consequences of his action. [12]

The same guide has been expressed frequently in corporate
statements of policies. One of the oldest of these is the
policy statement of Armco Steel Corporation, adopted in
1919. In part it reads:

> 1. To do business guided and governed by the
> highest standards of conduct and ethics, striving
> always for that sort of an ending in all things affect-
> ing the conduct of the business as would make "repu-
> tation" an invaluable and permanent asset. [13]

Kaiser Aluminum and Chemical Corporation has embodied
this same guide of individual integrity in a statement of
ethical policy for purchasing:

> All purchasing personnel will adhere to the
> highest standards of integrity and personal conduct

---

[12] Francis X. Sutton, Seymour E. Harris, Carl Kaysen, and James
Tobin, The American Business Creed (Cambridge, Mass.: Harvard
University Press, 1956), p. 251.

[13] Towle, op. cit., p. 267.

and thereby maintain and promote our reputation as an outstanding company with which to do business. [14]

THE MIDDLE NORMS

Henry M. Oliver has observed that what is most lacking in the present structure of ethical norms for business is a set of middle principles. [15]   There is wide agreement as to the nature of the ultimate moral truths expressed in the primary guides, but it is the application of these truths to the circumstances of the business environment which seems to be missing. Probably, as Oliver views the situation, the following guides fit his description of middle principles. These guides, while remaining theoretical, nevertheless are more specific than the primary guides; and by this reason to some degree they are more controversial.

THE GUIDE OF OFFICIAL LEGISLATION

Ethical conduct by executives requires observance of legislation imposed by legitimate civil authority.

Relation to the Primary Guides. This fourth guide is an application of the primary guide of support of social institutions. The legal structure of a given society expresses the specific and concrete acts to which citizens are obliged for the support and furtherance of basic social institutions which society as a whole has accepted.   Laws in this respect are initiated and enacted to reinforce the basic social institutions which are prevalent in a given society.   Thus a commitment to the social institutions of a given society necessarily implies a concomitant commitment to the embodiment of these social institutions as they are found in statutes.

---

[14] Ibid., pp. 273-74.

[15] Henry M. Oliver, "Trends Toward a New Moral Philosophy for Business," Business Horizons, I(2): 41, Spring, 1958.

Meaning of the Guide. The guide as expressed above calls for the observance of the law in the conduct of the business-man. It does not prohibit opposition to the law by legal means, such as lobbying for its removal or amendment, or for legislation which is more in accord with the convictions or the persuasions of the businessman. It is undoubtedly true that many laws in our statutes seem to impose restrictions which some businessmen feel are detrimental to a well-functioning free-enterprise system. They feel the need to work intelligently toward the revision of such laws. This is, of course, the legitimate manner of modifying or changing laws in a democratic society; and such activity should not be regarded as in opposition to the present guide. What the present guide does proscribe is a deliberate and intentional violation of a law which has been legitimately enacted.

Special consideration must be given to the case in which there is widespread disregard of a particular law by the general populace. In some cases, this disregard is condoned and even tacitly approved by civil authorities. In such cases, care needs to be exercised in the application of the present guide. The businessman should not be bound by what is generally recognized to be an inoperable law. In such cases he should be at liberty to follow what is the customary practice in his area. A case in point might be certain "blue laws" which are still in the statutes of several states. Such laws frequently prohibit the operation of business establishments on Sundays or certain religious holidays. Often such laws are generally disregarded; and, indeed, the case can sometimes be made that strict observance of the law could lead to a widespread social disutility. If amusement and entertainment firms could not operate on such days, much of the purpose of the day would be defeated.

Yet if such cases do provide an exception to the literal interpretation of this guide, it is important to note that this exception does not provide an escape hatch from civil obedience which the individual businessman can open up at will. The criterion for determining the applicability of this excuse from civil obedience does not rest in the private judgment of the individual businessman. Rather, the criterion is the objective and known fact that the law is presently not enforced by the civil authority. If such a condition is verified, it would seem to impose a grave and inappropriate burden on the businessman to exact from him a strict observance of such a law. But it is not for the individual businessman to decide whether or not he is to observe each particular law. This guide affirms the moral obligation of executives to observe laws even though they consider them in need of modification or repeal.

A more difficult situation occurs in the case of a law whose precise meaning or application is doubtful. Does the present guide bind the executive to obedience to such a doubtful law? In his observance of the law, must he avoid any action which might conceivably be considered a violation of the law? For instance, in the observance of federal antitrust laws, must the executive avoid any type of activity which is not certainly permitted by such legislation? The present researcher is of the opinion that such a demand would put an excessively and intolerably severe burden on the shoulders of the executive. There are many instances in which there have been strong disagreements between Justice Department officials and corporate lawyers concerning the legality of certain mergers. Often enough the courts have vindicated the opinions of the corporate lawyers. Thus another clarification of this guide is necessary. Where there is a genuine doubt by competent men concerning the meaning or application of the law, the executive should not be bound to follow the strictest interpretation of the law, but should be free to act in either direction as long as he is willing to abide by subsequent clarification of the judicial branch of government.

Support of the Guide in the Present Study. Religious values implicitly support this norm. Within the context of the Protestant values, observance of legitimate legislation is fundamental to personal honesty and integrity, explicit components of the Protestant ethic. From a viewpoint of Jewish values, the guide is probably more closely related to the concept of social order than to personal honesty. Study of the law (Torah), it was observed, was basic to the concept of the Jewish people as the chosen people of God. By observing law (first the law of God, and later legitimate civil law), the individual Jew shares in the religious heritage of his people.

The empirical investigation provides strong evidence that executives support this guide, though, as was observed previously, the respondents reserved to themselves the right to judge the relevance of the law to concrete circumstances. In four cases relating to the legal system, A (electrical-equipment price fixing), F (padding the expense account), E (use of inferior materials in a construction contract) and S (campaign bribe in exchange for a contract award), the executives were in relative agreement concerning support of the law. In two cases (C, use of insider information, and I, concealment of a bribe in an auditor's report), the executives manifested balanced disagreement concerning the obligation to support the law. Of these two cases, Case I seemed to represent a situation in which literal obedience of the law would work a real injustice; hence the judgment of the respondents was probably that the incident represented a legitimate exception to the law. This leaves only Case C in possible conflict with the guide of support of legitimate legislation, and in this case the damage to society could be judged remote and small compared to the immediate and catastrophic effects of choosing the alternative. [16]

Applications of the Guide. In a number of areas this guide might provide ethical direction to the confused businessman. The recent electrical-equipment price conspiracy is a case in point. [17] Here the executives of several large firms found themselves faced with a very difficult dilemma. They were faced with the choice of deliberately violating the law by entering illegal price agreements with competitors or avoiding such illegal tactics and facing a chaotic price situation (cutthroat competition) which would result in considerable damage to the majority of companies in their industry. One who reads an account of their problems can sympathize with the difficulty of their position. Indeed, there is a history of government intervention and market control simply to avoid the kind of evils which these companies faced. Nevertheless, their decision deliberately and knowingly to violate the law in order to maintain a viable (and profitable) situation for their own companies clearly runs counter to the norm under discussion.

---

[16]These cases were discussed at length above, p. 101, and following.

[17]Smith, op. cit. , pp. 132 et ff.

The National Electrical Manufacturers' Association has given apt expression to the values of this guide in the Preamble of its <u>Statement of Principles</u>:

> It is the responsibility and privilege of the members of the business community, as it is of all citizens, to observe the laws of the land. While all men, and all organizations, have the right to petition the Congress for a change in the laws, no man, and no organization, has a right to substitute individual judgments for those principles of behavior which are to be found in the law. Any other course can lead only to a collapse of order and to a deterioration of that system of government by law which is the foundation-stone of the United States. [18]

THE GUIDE OF REPRESENTATIVE AUTHORITY

Ethically responsible executives recognize their power and authority as representative, i. e. , held in the interest of others.

Meaning of the Guide. Chester I. Barnard showed considerable discernment when he observed that:

> One of the most important, if not dominant, characteristics of modern Western society, as contrasted with ancient, or with Western societies of one hundred or two hundred years [ago] , is the extent to which concrete behavior of individuals has become representative rather than personal. [19]

This is especially true of business society. The pervasiveness of this representative character in executive activity can hardly be exaggerated. The executive, as leader of a highly complex organization, exercises his authority in behalf of interests other than his own. Management authority in this respect has the fundamental character of trusteeship, and the executive himself the character of a trustee who acts in accordance with the aims or goals of others.

---

[18] Quoted in Towle, <u>op. cit.</u> , p. 277.

[19] Barnard, "Elementary Conditions of Business Morals, " p. 6.

This representative character of modern executive activity is especially significant with reference to the ethical parameters of business decisions. While the personal element can never be divorced from the executive process, nevertheless, it is precisely by reason of his official capacity as representative of the organization that the executive acts. Indeed, Barnard asserts that "every act of a trustee, director, officer, or employee is officially representative action."[20] In such a capacity, decisions motivated solely by personal advantage or gain, especially if adverse to representative interests, are inconsistent with the responsibilities which the executive assumes when he accepts a management position with a business concern.

The present guide attempts to express the proper relationship between personal and representative interests of the executive. It is important to recognize on the theoretical level the twofold aspect of every executive decision. With regard to its personal aspect, the executive needs to consider the demands of personal integrity, and it is hard to see how any action in violation of such integrity can be regarded as ethical. But consideration of this aspect is not enough. Further limitations may be imposed upon executive conduct by the fact of trusteeship, by reason of accountability for other legitimate interests, and by conflicts between competing interests of the business enterprise.

Support of the Guide in Present Research. Both the historical and empirical phases of the present research lend support to the guide of representative authority. The concept of trusteeship, common to both Protestant and Jewish value systems, approaches the guide inasmuch as it affirms the manager may not exercise power and control of wealth solely for personal advantage. While modern theories of representative authority have attempted to spell out who are the beneficiaries of this trusteeship relationship, these theories remain but applications of a value concept common to both Protestant and Jewish religious faiths.

Empirical evidence also tends to confirm the presence of this guide in the value standards of contemporary business executives. Most of the cases relevant to this guide

---

[20]Barnard, loc. cit.

are within the social responsibility scale.[21]   By consider-
ing such cases as W (executive's community activities), V
(hiding a plant shutdown from employees), and P (corporate
contributions to colleges), it is possible to discern an
implicit support of this guide.

Applications of the Guide.   Central to this guide is the question
of whom management represents in its official capacity.
Unfortunately, there is no consensus in responding to the
question, and thus it must be admitted that the guide, in its
present state of development, leaves much to be desired.

A number of scholars see management's main role in
the guardianship of stockholder rights and in the protection
of stockholder interests.[22]   Stockholders with the legal
vestiges of private ownership are regarded as the true
masters of the corporation.   It is they who approve the
broad objectives of the enterprise, select the officers, and
through their board of directors, control in some detail the
more important corporate policies.   And it is in the name
of the stockholders that the corporate executives act. Their
responsibility is to represent these stockholder interests.
Chiefly, this responsibility is fulfilled by means of directing
corporate policy toward the financial benefit of stockholders, but even this goal is deceptively simple.   Whether
stockholder benefit is best achieved by profit objectives,
dividend objectives, or by the maximization of the present
worth of stockholder investment is still an unsettled
question.

Other scholars have insisted that the representative
character of management implies that they need to look to
much more than stockholder interests alone.   Thus Richard
Eells[23] has enumerated the categories of contributor-
claimants whose interests are to be protected by management.   Besides stockholders, these claimants include

---

[21]Cases included in this scale are listed on p. 89.

[22]J. A. Livingston, The American Stockholder (Philadelphia: J. B.
Lippincott, Inc. , 1958), passim. See also Louis O. Kelso and Mortimer
J. Adler, The Capitalist Manifesto (New York: Random House, 1958),
pp. 77-94.

[23]Richard Eells, The Meaning of Modern Business (New York:
Columbia University Press, 1960). Cf. especially Chapter X: "Claimants on the Corporation, " pp. 211-16.

customers, employees, suppliers, competitors, the business community as a whole, local communities, and finally the general public.[24]   The manager, according to this theory, becomes a balancer of interests, a representative of several heterogeneous groups, and arbitrator and a judge of conflicting claims.   Indeed, Adolph A. Berle, Jr., and Gardiner C. Means seem to suggest that the manager needs to divide the income of the corporation among its claimants according to some idea of public welfare rather than according to stockholder interest:

> [It] seems almost essential if the corporate system is to survive, that the "control" of the great corporations should develop into a purely neutral technocracy, balancing a variety of claims by various groups in the community and assigning to each a portion of the income stream as the basis of public policy rather than private cupidity.[25]

While it may be too early to settle in a definitive manner this controversy, the present writer feels that there is a middle ground between these two positions.   Without going so far as to regard the corporation as a "constellation of interests,"[26] it is possible to recognize that different groups have some legitimate stakes in corporate policies. To a certain degree the manager needs to respect the interests of several classes of claimants. As Chester I. Barnard has remarked:

> The responsibilities of corporations, aside from the obligation to conform to their charters and to the law, are of two kinds: (1) those which may be called internal, relating to the equitable interests of the stockholders, creditors, directors, officers, and employees; and (2) those relating to the interests of

---

[24]Ibid., pp. 213-15.

[25]Adolph A. Berle, Jr., and Gardiner C. Means, The Modern Corporation and Private Property (New York: The Macmillan Company, 1932), p. 356.

[26]Cf. Richard Eells and Clarence Walton, Conceptual Foundations of Business (Homewood, Ill.: Richard D. Irwin, Inc., 1961), pp. 147-71.

competitors, communities, government, and society in general.[27]

At the same time, this writer feels it necessary to recognize in corporate decisions a primacy of stockholder interests. After the basic responsibility to conform to the corporation charter and to the law, the corporate officer needs to recognize that his trusteeship is held in the name of the stockholder and that in his official capacity he needs to give high priority to the stockholder interests. Far from simply distributing the income stream among various claimants according to his concept of equity, the manager must be fully cognizant of the legal position of the stockholder, who has an exclusive title to all net income. It must be remembered that it is the basic function of business to produce economic goods. This it could not do without stockholder investment. Thus it would seem that the legal position of the stockholder is supported by the simple exigencies of investment market: Without an exclusive claim to the net income of the corporation, the stockholder would be unwilling to risk his capital in business venture. Thus, as trustee, the manager may be called upon to look to the long-term interests of the stockholder rather than to short-run profit-maximization. He may even see stockholder benefits in the investment of corporate funds in non-business activities such as Community Chest contributions or civic-improvement programs. Such contributions may indeed actually contribute to profit-maximizing objectives, for the recognition of the legitimate claims of others on the corporation and the treatment of such claimants with equity and empathy often have a business-getting and business-retaining effect. Nevertheless, this writer believes that even such contributions as these need to be regarded as investments, or at least as expenditures made in the name of ownership interests. It is believed that this position differs from the Berle and Means opinion inasmuch as here it is suggested that the surplus created by the corporation is not to be regarded as an unattached fund to be divided among worthy claimants, but rather is to be regarded as the property of ownership interests, to be used in their name and for their interest.

---

[27]Barnard, "Elementary Conditions of Business Morals," p. 7.

This discussion should suggest that the guide of representative authority has not yet been sufficiently clarified to describe precisely the total breadth of executive responsibilities. Yet it is believed that it can, even in its present state of tentative formulation, provide a useful guide to ethical action. At least, as Robert W. Austin has observed, [28] inasmuch as it proscribes executive activity which is exclusively directed toward the executive's own personal and private benefit at the cost of company objectives, the guide provides a valuable rule. The executive who uses his position for his own personal interests without any regard for stockholder interest is certainly acting in a way which is repugnant to both the Livingston and the Eells positions.

Another contemporary problem of business philosophy is closely related to this guide. This problem concerns the legitimacy of business power, a subject which has been so much the concern of Adolf A. Berle, Jr., in recent years. [29] Berle finds the justification of the present power structure of American business in the fact that it exists by the public consensus, i. e., that the general public sees that business power is being used to meet the economic needs of the country as a whole. And this public consensus as expressed by widespread approval of the American private-enterprise system would immediately cease to exist if management lost its representative character. Paul Harbrecht [30] has carried this concept even further to state as a general social law that economic power will tend to gravitate toward those who will use it in a representative manner for the common benefit. Thus these authors related the legitimacy of business power to its representative character. It is quite possible, then, that this guide of representative authority will become the subject of intensified

---

[28] Robert W. Austin, quoted in "A Positive Code of Ethics," Business Week, June 17, 1961, p. 166.

[29] Adolph A. Berle, Jr., Economic Power and the Free Society (Santa Barbara: Center for the Study of Democratic Institutions, 1957); see also Power Without Property (New York: Harcourt, Brace and Company, 1959).

[30] Paul Harbrecht, S. J., Toward the Paraproprietal Society (New York: The Twentieth Century Fund, 1960), 45 pp.

scrutiny as the parameters of business philosophy are explored further.

THE GUIDE OF PARITY BETWEEN AUTHORITY AND MORAL RESPONSIBILITY

Moral responsibility is coextensive with authority; that is, in his decision-making capacity, an executive is morally responsible for all the effects of his decisions within his control.

Meaning of the Guide.   Keith Davis has observed [31] that the idea of power and responsibility going hand in hand is as old as civilization itself.   Responsibility in this context has reference to the obligation to use such power in a manner beneficial to all over whom it is exercised.   First expressions of the relationship between these two ideas were probably found in the political area, where authority to rule was coupled with responsibility to raise taxes, levy troops, and provide for the peace.   Indeed, it might be argued that the very understanding of the terms of power and responsibility leads to the conclusion that they are coextensive. Responsibility without power is unreasonable; power without responsibility is despotic or arbitrary.

One of the most significant contributions of management theory has been to spell out the application of this idea to the organizational relationships within the individual business firm.   The principle of parity of authority and responsibility as it has been expressed in management theory is fundamental to basic departmentation, the assignment of activities, the delegation of authority, and the function of control. [32]   No small number of organization deficiencies can undoubtedly be traced to the failure to heed the basic relationships described by this principle.   The exaction of responsibility without corresponding authority and the acceptance of authority without the corresponding recognition of responsibility still remain frequent in many business concerns.

---

[31] Keith Davis, "Can Business Afford to Ignore Social Responsibilities?" California Management Review, II(3): 71, Spring, 1960.

[32] Koontz and O'Donnell, op. cit., Chapters 13, 14, and 17.

Support of the Guide in the Present Study.   Even a limited treatment of the Protestant, Jewish, and Catholic faiths reveals
that the value embodied in the present guide is shared by
these religious traditions. The Protestant ethic, as has
been seen, reflects this value in the concept of the stewardship of wealth. The individual who has achieved the possession of economic wealth, or authority over its use, must
regard his wealth and authority as held in trust to be used
for the benefit of all society.[33] Though the Jewish religious tradition also shares the concept of stewardship of
wealth, the basis of the present guide is also closely related
to the value of Zedakah discussed in Chapter 2.[34] Personal
responsibility for action has been associated with the recognition of the individual's role as a member of society;
and, consequently, more is expected of the individual who
has authority or wealth than is expected of his less fortunate neighbor.[35]   Catholic tradition also supports this
guide through the concept of the social aspect of property.

The empirical study of the present work does not directly manifest the presence of this guide among the values
accepted by the respondents.   Indeed, since the guide
expresses a coextensiveness of two somewhat abstract
concepts, it would be conceptually difficult to devise an
empirical instrument which would verify such a guide.
However, the questionnaire does give some indication that
this guide would not be repugnant to a good number of the
respondents. In Case T, 96 of the respondents approved of
the use of company funds for the purchase of an expensive
chemical filter.   In Case V, the executives (91 percent)
disapproved of hiding a plant shutdown from employees.
Without attempting a measure of their willingness to affirm
the coextensiveness of authority and responsibility, these
cases seem to point to some degree of parallelism.

Applications of the Guide. The application of this principle to
the area of business morality seems both necessary and

---

[33]See Kenneth E. Boulding's expression of this viewpoint in "Our
Lost Economic Gospel, " The Christian Century, LXVII (33) (August
16, 1950), p. 970. Quoted in Chapter 1, p. 21.

[34]Cf. Chapter 2, pp. 35 and following.

[35]Cf. Chapter 2, pp. 42-43.

reasonable. Indeed, the affirmation of the existence of individual responsibility is a frequent ingredient of business creeds. [36] What is often lacking in these creeds is the precise statement of the coextensiveness of this responsibility with effective power. It is, in effect, an extension or an application of the primary guide of personal integrity. For if an individual recognizes the need for moral consistency in his activities, he will see the relationship between his own actions and the results of those actions.

The full implications of this guide must not be overlooked. It is deceptively simple. Most managers would probably accept its logic; the problems come in its application to specific issues. Business decisions have such a pervasive influence that it has been argued that the acceptance of total responsibility for all the effects of business decisions will so complicate the process of decision making that management is likely to lose its effectiveness. [37] Theodore Levitt, for example, in his argument against social responsibilities, has made the point that if business is to become involved in all the noneconomic dimensions of its decisions, it will lose its vitality as a profit-making and economizing institution:

> The power which the corporation gains as a sort of demi-church it will lose as an agency of profit-motive capitalism. Indeed, as the profit motive becomes increasingly sublimated, capitalism will become only a shadow—the torpid remains of creative dynamism which was and might have been. [38]

Benjamin Selekman[39] has also voiced a fear that the assumption of a wide variety of noneconomic responsibilities will debilitate the main objective of all business activity, which he sees as the efficient provision of goods and services to society.

---

[36]Sutton et al., op. cit., pp. 251-55.

[37]Bernard Nossiter, "The Troubled Conscience of American Business," Harper's Magazine, 227(1,360): 42, September, 1963.

[38]Theodore Levitt, "The Dangers of Social Responsibility," Harvard Business Review, XXXVI(5): 46, September-October, 1958.

[39]Benjamin M. Selekman, A Moral Philosophy for Business (New York: McGraw-Hill Book Company, 1959), especially Chapter 27.

These opinions at first glance appear as serious objections to the guide expressed above; and, indeed, they do point to a fundamental controversy in current business literature. It may be that considerably more research is needed before this guide can achieve complete acceptance. Nevertheless, there are a number of business authorities who respond to the opinions above by suggesting that a rejection of responsibility for noneconomic aspects of business decisions will ultimately result in the public withdrawal of business power.[40] More precisely, it is frequently argued that if businessmen reject these noneconomic considerations, government legislation will effectively check business power in such areas. Thus Admiral Ben Moreell, former Chairman of the Board of Jones and Laughlin Steel Corporation, has put it this way:

> I am convinced that unless we do accept social responsibilities, the vacuum created by our unwillingness will be filled by those who would take us down the road to complete statism and inevitable moral and social collapse.[41]

This controversy represents a wide split in the business community—one which cannot be resolved here. However, the point of interest is that the defense of social responsibilities for business has taken the direction of the defense of the guide now under discussion. And it becomes apparent that, while the guide may lack universal acceptance, there are many who feel that one of the most vital controversies of business morality is now being fought precisely in the area of this guide.

THE GUIDE OF THE PRIVATE ENTERPRISE

Support of social institutions in the United States includes support of private enterprise as a legitimate and essential system of economic organization.

The Meaning of the Guide. The private-enterprise system, with its focus on the profit motive, has been characterized as

---

[40]Davis, op. cit. , pp. 73-74.

[41]Quoted in ibid. , p. 73.

the most productive economic system known to modern man. [42] But apart from the case for the economic superiority of private enterprise, it may also be regarded as a social value which is supported by a large majority of the American people.   In this respect it is related to the first primary guide of social institutions; and, therefore, its support takes on a moral character. Because the American people are so strongly committed to private enterprise as a social value, the businessman himself needs to support it as a basic social value.

Undoubtedly, this commitment is rooted in a respect for the individual.   It is not just that the individual, when motivated by the opportunity to make a profit, will produce more efficiently.   Even more important is the belief that society is an institution whose major objective is to further the welfare of its members, and this welfare is achieved, at least in part, by providing the individual with the freedom and the opportunity to seek his own betterment through his own private industry.   Private enterprise, in this respect, is intimately bound up with the American concept of liberty and human dignity.

Support of the Guide in the Present Study.   Much has been written on the relationship of the Protestant, Hebrew, and Catholic faiths to the private-enterprise system.   Indeed, the first two chapters of the present work investigate the contributions of Max Weber and Werner Sombart, who defend a holy alliance between religion and capitalism; and the whole of these chapters may be considered as support for the present guide.   Nevertheless, the present writer thinks it important to note that the value of this guide is not primarily a religious one, but rather it is a value economic and political in nature. Especially in the case of this guide, the implication that a religious influence explains the existence of this value must carefully be avoided.   Certainly religious faith has been part of the Weltanschauung in which the private-enterprise system has flourished.   It would be equally erroneous to deny any influence to religious factors in the evolution of the private-enterprise system as it

---

[42]This is a commonly held opinion, though one which has been challenged with some merit. Cf. Henry Wallich, The Cost of Freedom (New York: Harper and Brothers, 1960), p. 40 and following.

would be to ascribe to these religious factors the total influence. The true measure of their influence must lie between these extremes.

It is likewise difficult to find specific confirmation of this guide in the empirical section of the present study. Rather than being the object of a specific set of cases, support of the private-enterprise system seems to run through the whole questionnaire as a fundamental supposition. Indeed, acceptance of this guide by the vast majority of businessmen is so apparent that it needs no specific empirical confirmation in the present work. [43]

Application of the Guide. This guide suggests an inclination or mood which should be found in an executive rather than a hard-fast, concrete law. What it implies is that the businessman should show a propensity to favor the private-enterprise system as the most suitable means of providing economic goods and services in the American environment. Only when there is reasonable evidence that some particular public need cannot be satisfied by private enterprise should the businessman advocate government intervention in the private-enterprise system. Such governmental influence should be based on a need which is unable to be met by private initiative. And when such intervention is necessary, it should be of such a character as to affect least the individual-business-enterprise system.

George Steiner has proposed a similar guide as a principle to be considered in introducing new economic controls into the American economy. He views the private-enterprise system as a fundamental commitment which is almost unanimously accepted by the American people. Thus governmental economic controls need to take cognizance of it as a basic social value. As he expresses and explains this principle:

> The control should be instituted within the framework of the basic institutions of the individual enterprise system. This principle, of course, is anchored in the fundamental policy commitment which

---

[43] If desired, a more explicit and comprehensive treatment of the acceptance of the private-enterprise system by the business community can be found in Sutton et al. , op. cit. , Chapters 3, 4, and 8.

the American people almost unanimously accept to preserve the basic institutions of the present-day economic system. It means . . . that controls ought not subvert the institution of private property, freedom of consumer choice, freedom of choosing an occupation, the profit motive, individual incentives, and so on. [44]

And Robert W. Austin has included support of the profit motive as among the four principles embodied in his code of conduct for executives. He expresses the businessman's commitment to the profit motive in the following words:

The professional business manager affirms that when business managers follow this code of conduct, the profit motive is the best incentive for the development of a sound, expanding, and dynamic economy. [45]

SUMMARY OF THE CHAPTER

The present chapter has attempted to formulate a tentative statement of ethical guides for businessmen. These guides are based on an objective study of the business environment from both an historical and an empirical methodology. In the present study these guides are proposed as theoretical norms generally suitable to give ethical direction to executives in concrete decision-making situations. However, the guides remain broad in content, and considerable judgment is needed in the application of these guides to particular circumstances.

---

[44] George A. Steiner, Government's Role in Economic Life (New York: McGraw-Hill Book Company, 1953), p. 395.

[45] Robert W. Austin, "Code of Conduct for Executives, " Harvard Business Review, XXXIX(5): 60, September-October, 1961.

QUESTIONNAIRE

1. Instructions: Please check the alternative which best expresses your ethical judgment of the following cases:

   A. Recently a number of high-ranking executives of several electrical companies were convicted and sentenced to jail for conspiring to fix the prices of heavy electrical-equipment products. Their defense counsel argued that while their action was technically illegal, they sought to rationalize a chaotic pricing situation. What is your evaluation of the action of these executives?

approve	_____	5-1*
somewhat approve	_____	2
somewhat disapprove	_____	3
disapprove	_____	4

   B. John Saxor is the Pacific Coast Sales Representative of Ajax Tool Company. He has been instructed by his superior, Mr. Bruce Maynard, Vice-President of Sales, to adopt a sales policy Saxor considers unethical. Mr. Maynard and Saxor have discussed the policy at length, and it is apparent Maynard thinks the policy is quite ethical. He orders Saxor to follow the policy, and Saxor reluctantly does so. What is your opinion of Saxor's action?

approve	_____	6-1
somewhat approve	_____	2
somewhat disapprove	_____	3
disapprove	_____	4

---

*Figures used for coding the questionnaire. (Numbers 1-4 were reserved for punch-card identification of the test group.)

C.   Lawrence Stone, a member of the Board of Directors of Scott Electronics Corporation, has just
learned that the company is about to announce a
2-for-1 stock split and an increase of dividends.
Stone personally is on the brink of bankruptcy. A
quick gain of a few thousand dollars can save him
from economic and social ruin. He decides to take
advantage of this information concerning the stock
split by purchasing stock now to sell in a few days
at a profit.

approve	_____	7-1
somewhat approve	_____	2
somewhat disapprove	_____	3
disapprove	_____	4

D.   James Sherman sells used cars for Harrison Auto
Company. Although he feels that the cars he sells
are reasonably priced for the market, in his sales
talk he is forced to match the extravagant claims
and tactics of his competitors. The company en-
gages in such practices as setting back speedometers, superficially hiding major defects, and
putting pressure on prospects to close a deal on
their first visit. Sherman knows that the company
could not survive without such practices; yet he
personally feels repugnance toward them. Nevertheless he follows these practices.

approve	_____	8-1
somewhat approve	_____	2
somewhat disapprove	_____	3
disapprove	_____	4

E.   The Reed Engineering Company faces a very competitive situation in bidding for a contract to con-
struct a new store for a large discount chain.
Inasmuch as the company is seriously in need of
the work, A. Wallis Jennings, one of the partners
in the company, suggests that Reed submit a bid
which will certainly be low, and then make its
margin on the use of inferior materials. Jennings
is certain this can be done without arousing the
suspicion of building inspectors. Jennings argues
that any company which is awarded the contract

will have to do that since the bidding will be so
competitive. Mr. Elwood Reed, senior partner in
the company, agrees that it will be necessary to do
this. He observes that it is not an infrequent
practice anyway.

approve	_____	9-1
somewhat approve	_____	2
somewhat disapprove	_____	3
disapprove	_____	4

F. Brian George is a salesman for Sweet Soap Company. With commissions, his salary usually
comes to about $12,000 per year. George usually
supplements this to the extent of about $600 per
year by changing certain unauthorized personal
expenses against his expense account. He feels
that this is a common practice in his company; and
if everybody else is doing it, he doesn't see why
he shouldn't do it also.

approve	_____	10-1
somewhat approve	_____	2
somewhat disapprove	_____	3
disapprove	_____	4

G. Wallace Brown, Treasurer of Lloyd Enterprises,
is about to retire and contemplates recommending
one of his two assistants for promotion to Treasurer. Brown is sure that his recommendation will
be accepted, but he also knows that the assistant
not recommended will find his promotion opportunities seriously limited. One of the assistants,
William Grimes, seems to him the most qualified
for the new assignment, but the other assistant,
John Leonard, is the nephew of the president of
Lloyd's biggest customer. Though Brown hates to
do it, he recommends Leonard for the job because
he feels his relationship with his uncle will help
Lloyd's.

approve	_____	11-1
somewhat approve	_____	2
somewhat disapprove	_____	3
disapprove	_____	4

H. Mr. Irving Kraft, editor of the Diamond City Daily
    News is troubled. He has just received a visit
    from Mr. Raymond Cramer, a public relations
    executive with the Aztec Department Store. Aztec
    is a big advertiser in the Daily News, and its con-
    tinued purchase of advertising space is very im-
    portant to the paper. Recently the department
    store sold a large quantity of electrical appliances
    which proved defective and refused to exchange the
    merchandise for better quality appliances. The
    Daily News at the present time is running a series
    of articles on local business firms. Mr. Cramer
    wants to be sure that a story on the Aztec Depart-
    ment Store will contain no mention of this unfor-
    tunate occurrence. Mr. Kraft is troubled; but in
    order not to offend this important advertiser, he
    agrees not to mention the sale of the defective
    appliances.

              approve   _____ 12-1
              somewhat approve   _____   2
              somewhat disapprove   _____   3
              disapprove   _____   4

I. Robert Schall and Company, Public Accountants,
    have been called in to audit the books of the Lake-
    wood Trucking Company in anticipation of a public
    sale of stock. In the course of the audit Mr. Schall
    discovers an item that leaves him puzzled: a
    $20,000 advertising expense paid to the Chicago
    Advertising Company. This was a one-payment
    expense three years ago, and no further business
    has been done with the Chicago firm. When ques-
    tioned by Mr. Schall, Mr. Clarence Wallen, Presi-
    dent of the trucking company, readily admits this
    money was used as a bribe to pay a union official.
    "It was a question of paying up or going out of
    business," Mr. Wallen explains. Since the com-
    pany has now been unionized by a reputable union,
    Mr. Wallen sees no possibility of this situation
    recurring. He asks Mr. Schall to make no mention
    of this in his Auditor's Report. Since the firm

seems soundly managed in every other respect,
Mr. Schall agrees to Mr. Wallen's request.

approve	_____	13-1
somewhat approve	_____	2
somewhat disapprove	_____	3
disapprove	_____	4

J. Howard Piser, President of Piser Fashions Co.,
has heard rumors that a competitor, Sunset Fashions, is coming out with a new line of spring styles
which in all likelihood will sweep the market.
Piser cannot afford to wait until the new styles
come out, so he hires Robert Bishop, plant supervisor of Sunset. Although Mr. Bishop is not a
designer, in his capacity of plant supervisor he
has become thoroughly familiar with the new Sunset line. It is understood that Mr. Bishop will
make known to his new employer the full details of
the new Sunset styles.

approve	_____	14-1
somewhat approve	_____	2
somewhat disapprove	_____	3
disapprove	_____	4

K. Richard Cobb is a salesman for Lester and Brad-
dock, stockbrokers. He has been instructed to
recommend to his customers some Central Elec-
tric Power Co. bonds, as the brokerage firm is
carrying a heavy inventory in these bonds at the
present time. Cobb does not feel the bonds are a
good investment under present circumstances;
and he is reluctant to recommend them. However,
after some thought, he decides to follow the company directive and recommend the bonds.

approve	_____	15-1
somewhat approve	_____	2
somewhat disapprove	_____	3
disapprove	_____	4

L. Recently "Big Steel" has been criticized for not
using every means at its disposal to ease racial
tensions in Birmingham. In particular, it was
contended that U.S. Steel should exert pressure

for integration by letting banks and suppliers know that it would give more business to those who favored better opportunities for Negroes. At a news conference, Chairman of the Board of U.S. Steel, Roger M. Blough, rejected such proposals and observed that corporation officials who are citizens in a community "can exercise what small influence they may have as citizens. But for a corporation to attempt to exert any kind of economic compulsion to achieve a particular end in the social area seems to be quite beyond what a corporation should do."

approve	_____	16-1
somewhat approve	_____	2
somewhat disapprove	_____	3
disapprove	_____	4

M. Jenkins Manufacturing Company is faced with the necessity of closing down one of its two Los Angeles plants. This will necessitate laying off about 100 employees. Another 100 employees will be transferred to the other plant in the same area. Though the company is not unionized, generous allowances have been set aside for separation pay. The problem which Mr. Howard Jenkins, company president, faces is whether to discharge older and more highly paid workers who have been with the company for a number of years, or the younger and less highly paid workers who have less seniority. The industry is a competitive one; and Mr. Jenkins is concerned about his company's ability to compete, so he decides to discharge the older employees.

approve	_____	17-1
somewhat approve	_____	2
somewhat disapprove	_____	3
disapprove	_____	4

N. The Dodd Textile Company makes shirts in a large western city. Because of the severity of competition, the company is forced to hire employees from immigrant and other underprivileged groups which accept substandard wages. Recently union officials have accused such plants as this as maintaining "sweatshop conditions." Lesley Smith, the owner, admits conditions are not ideal and that employees can hardly make sufficient wages for a minimum living standard; but, he says, he is at least providing some employment for people who would otherwise probably be unemployed. Further, he feels he's entitled to his own profits which he would not receive if he raised wages.

approve	_____ 18-1
somewhat approve	_____ 2
somewhat disapprove	_____ 3
disapprove	_____ 4

O.   The St. Clair Importing Company, a U. S. firm, wholly owns a Canadian subsidiary, the Montclair Importing Company. Montclair has been offered the opportunity to merchandise a number of products manufactured in Red China. The Chinese price of these products is so attractive that the Canadian firm estimates it will be able to increase substantially the usual markup and still sell the products at a retail price below Canadian prices. The U. S. firm has contacted the U. S. State Department; and while it would be illegal and against public policy for the American firm to market the products in the U. S., there is no prohibition for the Canadian subsidiary to sell them in Canada. The firm decides to complete negotiations and distribute the products through its Canadian subsidiary.

approve	_____ 19-1
somewhat approve	_____ 2
somewhat disapprove	_____ 3
disapprove	_____ 4

P.   The Wiley Electric Company has a program to help colleges in the U. S. It agrees to match the contribution of any of its employees to colleges of their choice. Recently objection has been made to this policy on the grounds that it is distributing stockholder funds without their consent. The company has responded to this objection by pointing out that by such a policy it is fulfilling its community obligations.

approve	_____	20-1
somewhat approve	_____	2
somewhat disapprove	_____	3
disapprove	_____	4

Q. Dean Joseph Maynard of Redwood University has approached Mr. Robert Schall of Robert Schall and Company, Public Accountants, and has requested him to take a small number of foreign students as accounting apprentices for the summer months. These men are graduate accounting students who lack any contact with practical business conditions in the U. S. After consulting his staff, Mr. Schall concludes that bringing such inexperienced men into the firm for such a short length of time will be a burden to the company's operation. He refuses the Dean's request but offers to speak to the students at the University.

approve	_____	21-1
somewhat approve	_____	2
somewhat disapprove	_____	3
disapprove	_____	4

R. Harry Ruckus, Vice-President of Westerly Chemical Company, feels that sending expensive Christmas gifts to customers compromises their position as buyers, and thus is a form of bribery. Yet he knows that this is a common practice among his competitors and that sales are likely to be adversely affected by failure to conform to the traditional practice. He decides to send the gifts.

approve	_____	22-1
somewhat approve	_____	2
somewhat disapprove	_____	3
disapprove	_____	4

S. The Kauffman Construction Company has just submitted a bid on a new city hall for Diamond City. Two days ago Mr. William Henderson, Assistant to the Mayor of Diamond City, visited the office of Mr. Karl Kauffman and hinted that his company would be awarded the bid if Mr. Kauffman was willing to contribute $10,000 to the Mayor's campaign for reelection. Kauffman needed this contract badly to keep his construction crews organized and working through the next few months, so he agreed to make the campaign contribution from the company funds.

approve	_____	23-1
somewhat approve	_____	2
somewhat disapprove	_____	3
disapprove	_____	4

T. Western Petroleum, Inc., has a large refinery located in the suburbs of a large California city. The company has for years burned the waste products at this plant as the most efficient means of waste disposal. Though there is an ordinance against burning rubbish in the area, the company was easily able to get an exemption for refinery operations. The burning of waste petroleum products does cause soot and odor to spread through neighboring housing tracts. Mr. Dudley Johnson, Vice-President of Production, suggests that the company install a filter which will reduce considerably the amount of impurities released by the disposal system. Though the cost of this filter is substantial and will noticeably reduce net income for several years, the company goes ahead with its installation.

approve	_____	24-1
somewhat approve	_____	2
somewhat disapprove	_____	3
disapprove	_____	4

U. Walter Preston, purchasing agent for Comfort Furniture Company, asks his friend William Nelson to become his partner in the establishment of a new firm. Preston suggests that they start a small trucking company to haul furniture from Comfort's suppliers to the company's main warehouse in Philadelphia. Preston, in his capacity as purchasing agent, will direct Comfort's suppliers to send their orders via the new freight firm.

Prices of the new firm will be competitive, but the certainty of a steady flow of freight will make the firm quite profitable. Nelson is to manage the trucking company while Preston stays with Comfort Furniture. Nelson wonders if such an arrangement is ethical, but finally agrees to the formation of the new firm.

approve	_____ 25-1
somewhat approve	_____ 2
somewhat disapprove	_____ 3
disapprove	_____ 4

V. The Board of Directors of the Boldt Manufacturing Company has decided to close down its Eastbrook plant in four months. The plant employs 200 workers in a Michigan town of 30,000. At a recent Board meeting, Paul Belcher, company Treasurer, has urged that the employees not be informed of this decision until the actual day of their dismissal. If this is not done, he argues, absenteeism and productivity declines will seriously hamper output. Henry Roscoe, Personnel Director, feels that the employees should be given some advance notice in order to plan necessary adjustments, even at the cost of absenteeism and productivity declines. Nevertheless, Roscoe is overruled, and the company keeps the plant shutdown a secret.

approve	_____ 26-1
somewhat approve	_____ 2
somewhat disapprove	_____ 3
disapprove	_____ 4

W. Brown Motor Company has been producing automobiles in Detroit for over twenty years. Though corporate responsibilities are heavy, Mr. James Wilhelm, President, has always spent some company-paid time in community activities and has encouraged his subordinates to do likewise. He recently summed up his philosophy on this subject in the following way: "It is no longer just enough to build a better mousetrap. Good industrial citizenship consists mainly in becoming a part of the community and cultivating genuinely friendly relationships with the people who live in it. A company can become too exclusively profit-oriented. ''

approve _____ 27-1
somewhat approve _____ 2
somewhat disapprove _____ 3
disapprove _____ 4

X. Big Productions, Inc. , produces a weekly TV program which stresses violence and brutality among juvenile gangs in the slum area of a large but unnamed American city. The program is very popular and receives high Nielsen ratings, but several community leaders have publicly criticized the program as contributing to juvenile delinquency. The company has argued that its function is to make and market a popular product, not to attempt to upgrade the moral values of society.

approve _____ 28-1
somewhat approve _____ 2
somewhat disapprove _____ 3
disapprove _____ 4

Y. In 1946, at the close of World War II, the major auto companies found themselves in a ''sellers' market,'' that is, for some months after postwar production was resumed, the demand for new cars exceeded the supply. Instead of selling the new cars for the high price the market would bear, the auto manufacturers rather set their prices considerably lower and aimed for a traditional pattern of gross margin on sales even though this meant less profit than was possible under the circumstances. What is your opinion of this decision of the auto manufacturers?

approve _____ 29-1
somewhat approve _____ 2
somewhat disapprove _____ 3
disapprove _____ 4

Z.   King Development Company has just purchased 1,000 acres of Arizona desert. The land, although in an undeveloped area, is only a few miles off the main highway between Phoenix and Tucson. The tract has been named "Desert Estates" and has been divided into 1-acre parcels. The company intends to sell these parcels by mail at $449 per acre. A well has been sunk on one parcel to prove the availability of water, and the development company also plans to bring electrical service to the site at its own expense. While advertisements will not be fraudulent, they will stress the potential appreciation of property values in Desert Estates.

approve	_____	30-1
somewhat approve	_____	2
somewhat disapprove	_____	3
disapprove	_____	4

2.   Rank (1-5) the following as qualities you would like to find in your associates:

_____ leadership	31
_____ hard work	32
_____ ability to get along with others	33
_____ thrift	34
_____ technical knowhow	35

3.   Rank (1-5) the following as qualities you would like to find in your associates:

_____ sensitivity to others	36
_____ honesty	37
_____ dedication to the organization	38
_____ breadth of interests	39
_____ judgment	40

4.   Rank (1-5) the following qualities according to their importance for business success:

_____ hard work	41
_____ family and social connections	42
_____ ability to get along with others	43
_____ dedication to the organization	44
_____ honesty	45

5. Which of the following men would you prefer to work with?

    a. Harry White: "I think that if a man joins a reputable company and then remains sensitive and responsive to the ethical values of his colleagues, he won't stray far from the ethical ideal. "

    b. Bob Easton: "I have some strong ethical commitments I've formulated through the years, and I'll resign before I compromise these principles. "

    White   _____ 46-1
    Easton   _____   2

6. Rank (1-6) the following according to their importance in influencing ethical conduct in business generally.

    _____ family training   47
    _____ conduct of superiors   48
    _____ conduct of peers   49

    _____ school and university training   50
    _____ religious training   51
    _____ practices in industry   52

7. What is the one unethical practice in your industry you would most like to see eliminated?

    53
    54

8. List some other practices in your industry you consider unethical:

    55
    56
    57

9. Below are listed some suggestions
    which have been proposed for the
    improvement of business ethics.
    What is your opinion of these sug-
    gestions?

	approve	somewhat approve	somewhat disapprove	disapprove	
a. Develop some widely accepted general principles of business ethics.					58
b. Introduce courses in Business Ethics in business schools.					59
c. Introduce industry codes of ethical practices.					60
d. Legislate stronger governmental regulation of business.					61
e. Encourage a more active participation of religious leaders in developing general ethical norms for business.					62

10. What suggestions would you make as effective means of
    improving business ethics?

                                                    63
                                                    64

11. Now, will you indicate the following information about
    yourself?

    a. Age: b. Sex:

        Under 30 years ____ 65-1   Male   ____66-1
               30-34   ____   2   Female____   2
               35-39   ____   3

               40-44   ____   4
               45-49   ____   5
               50-54   ____   6

               55-59   ____   7
               60-65   ____   8
        Over   65   ____   9

c.   Religion:

Protestant _____ 67-1   (please specify):_____
Catholic   _____   2

Jewish   _____   3
Other   _____   4   (please specify):_____

None   _____   5

d.   Formal education: e.   Name of
                                                     last
High school or less   _____ 68-1   school
Some college   _____   2   attended:
Bachelor's degree   _____   3
Some graduate studies   _____   4   _____69
M.A., M.B.A.,or higher   _____   5

f.   Income: From   Total (including
                          Salary   Income bonuses,
                                                   stock
                                                   options,
                                                   dividends,
Less than $5,000   _____ 70-1 _____ 71-1   rents,
$ 5,000- 7,499   _____   2 _____   2   interest,
   7,500- 9,999   _____   3 _____   3   etc.)

  10,000-14,999   _____   4 _____   4
  15,000-19,999   _____   5 _____   5
  20,000-24,999   _____   6 _____   6

  25,000-29,999   _____   7 _____   7
  30,000-39,999   8   8
  40,000-49,999   _____   9 _____   9

  50,000-59,999   _____   O _____   O
  60,000 or over   _____   X _____   X

g.   How often do you deal with your company's
     customers?

                    practically all of the time _____ 72-1
                    most of the time   _____   2
                    about half of the time   _____   3

                    some of the time   _____   4
                    hardly at all   _____   5
                    never   _____   6

h.   Approximate size of your company by volume of:

	Sales		Assets	
None	_____	73-1	_____	74-1
Less than $250,000	_____	2	_____	2
$250,000- 499,999	_____	3	_____	3
500,000- 999,999	_____	4	_____	4
1,000,000- 9,999,999	_____	5	_____	5
10,000,000- 49,999,999	_____	6	_____	6
50,000,000- 99,999,999	_____	7	_____	7
100,000,000- 499,999,999	_____	8	_____	8
500,000,000- 1,000,000,000	_____	9	_____	9
1,000,000,000- 5,000,000,000	_____	O	_____	O
Over 5,000,000,000	_____	X	_____	X

i.   Company size by number of employees:

1-49	_____	75-1
50-99	_____	2
100-249	_____	3
250-499	_____	4
500-999	_____	5
1,000-9,999	_____	6
10,000-19,999	_____	7
20,000 or more	_____	8

j.   How would you classify your position according to the following descriptions? (check one)

76-1 ___ Top management: chief executive officer and immediate subordinates.

2 ___ Front-line supervisory position: an administrative position which directly supervises or manages nonmanagers.

3 ___ Middle management: managers whose position in the organization falls between top management and front-line management.

76-4 ___ Nonmanage-   all others employed in
      ment   business.
      personnel:

5 ___ Professional: doctor, practicing lawyer,
                  practicing CPA, professor,
                  consultant, military offi-
                  cer, government official,
                  union official, clergyman,
                  and the like.

k. What is the title of your present position?

          _____ 77

l. What industry is your company engaged in?
    (Check one)

78-1 ___ Manufacturing consumer goods
   2 ___ Manufacturing industrial goods
   3 ___ Engineering, research, and development

   4 ___ Management consulting and business ser-
          vices
   5 ___ Banking, investment, insurance
   6 ___ Construction

   7 ___ Mining or extraction, oil
   8 ___ Retail or wholesale trade
   9 ___ Transportation, public utilities

   O ___ Advertising, media, publishing
   X ___ Consumer services
   y ___ Other (please specify)

m. How would you rate the competition in this
    industry?

very competitive	___	79-1
more than average	___	2
average	___	3
less than average	___	4
very little competition	___	5

A SELECTED BIBLIOGRAPHY OF BUSINESS ETHICS

BOOKS

Berle, Adolf A., Jr., The American Economic Republic. New York: Harcourt, Brace and World, Inc., 1963.

_____ , Power Without Property. New York: Harcourt, Brace and World, Inc., 1959.

Bowen, Howard R., Social Responsibilities of the Businessman. New York: Harper and Brothers, 1953.

Bunting, J. Whitney, (editor), Ethics for Modern Business Practice. New York: Prentice-Hall, Inc., 1953.

Childs, Marquis W., and Douglass Cater, Ethics In A Business Society. New York: Harper and Brothers, 1954.

Cleveland, Harlan, and Harold D. Lasswell, Ethics and Business. New York: Harper and Row, Inc., 1962.

Cronin, John F., S.S., Social Principles and Economic Life. Milwaukee: Bruce Publishing Co., 1959.

Dalton, Melville, Men Who Manage. New York: John Wiley and Sons, Inc., 1959.

Dempsey, Bernard, S.J., The Functional Economy. Englewood Cliffs, N.J.: Prentice-Hall, Inc., 1958.

Eells, Richard, The Meaning of Modern Business. New York: Columbia University Press, 1960.

_____ , and Clarence Walton, Conceptual Foundations of Business. Homewood, Ill.: Richard D. Irwin, Inc., 1961.

Garrett, Thomas M., S.J., Ethical Problems of American Advertising. Rome: The Gregorian University Press, 1961.

_____ , Ethics in Business. New York: Sheed and Ward, Inc., 1963.

Golembiewski, Robert T., Men, Management and Morality. New York: McGraw-Hill Book Co., 1962.

Hellerstein, Jerome R., Taxes, Loopholes and Morals. New York: McGraw-Hill Book Company, 1963.

Johnston, Herbert, Business Ethics. New York: Pitman Publishing Corp., 1961.

Leys, W.A.R., Ethics For Business Decisions. Englewood Cliffs: Prentice-Hall, Inc., 1960.

McGuire, Joseph W., Business and Society. New York: McGraw-Hill Book Co., Inc., 1963.

Mills, C. Wright, The Power Elite. New York: Oxford University Press, 1956.

Moody, Joseph N. and Justus George Lawler, (editors), The Challenge of Mater et Magistra. New York: Herder and Herder, 1963.

Moore, Wilbert E., The Conduct of the Corporation. New York: Random House, 1962.

Quinn, Francis X., S.J., (editor), Ethics, Advertising and Responsibility. Westminister, Md.: Canterbury Press, 1963.

Selekman, Benjamin M., A Moral Philosophy For Business. New York: McGraw-Hill Book Co., 1959.

Sharp, Frank Chapman, and Philip G. Fox, Business Ethics: Studies In Fair Competition. New York: D. Appleton Century Co., Inc., 1937.

Spurrier, William A., Ethics and Business. New York: Charles Scribner's Sons, 1963.

Sutton, Francis X., Seymour E. Harris, Carl Kaysen, and James Tobin, The American Business Creed. Cambridge, Mass.: Harvard University Press, 1956.

Thompson, Stewart, Management Creeds and Philosophies. New York: American Management Association, Inc., 1958.

Towle, Joseph W., (editor), Ethics and Standards in American Business. Boston: Houghton-Mifflin Co., 1964.

Warner, W. Lloyd, and James C. Abegglen, Big Business Leaders in America. New York: Harper and Brothers, 1955.

Wirtenberger, Henry J., S.J., Morality and Business. Chicago: Loyola University Press, 1962.

PERIODICALS

Adams, Walter, "Corporate Giantism, Ethics and the Public Interest," Review of Social Economy, 21 (March, 1963), 1-18.

Andlinger, Gerhard R., "The Crucible of Our Business Creeds," Business Horizons, 2 (Fall, 1959), 34-44.

Austin, Robert W., "Code of Conduct for Executives," Harvard Business Review, 39 (September-October, 1961), 53-61.

Barnard, Chester I., "Elementary Conditions of Business Morals," California Management Review, 1 (Fall, 1958), 1-13.

Baumhard, Raymond C., S. J., "How Ethical Are Businessmen?" Harvard Business Review, 39 (July-August, 1961), 6 ff.

Boulding, Kenneth E., "Religious Foundations of Economic Progress," Harvard Business Review, 30 (May-June, 1952), 33-40.

Broehl, Wayne G., Jr., "Insights Into Business and Society," Harvard Business Review, 44 (May-June, 1966), 6-37.

Cary, William L., "The Case For Higher Corporate Standards," Harvard Business Review, 40 (September-October, 1962), 53-9.

Cheit, Earl F., "Why Managers Cultivate Social Responsibility," California Management Review, 7 (Fall, 1964), 3-22.

Collier, Abram T., "Faith in a Creative Society," Harvard Business Review, 35 (May-June, 1957), 35-41.

Culliton, James W., "Business and Religion," Harvard Business Review, 27 (May, 1949), 265-71.

Davis, Keith, "Can Business Afford to Ignore Social Responsibilities?" California Management Review, 2 (Spring, 1960), 70-6.

Dempsey, Bernard W., S. J., "The Roots of Business Responsibility," Harvard Business Review, 27 (July, 1949), 393-404.

Farmer, Richard N., "The Ethical Dilemma of American Capitalism," California Management Review, 6 (Summer, 1964), 47-58.

Finkelstein, Louis, "The Businessman's Moral Failure," Fortune, 58 (September, 1958), 116 ff.

Frederick, William C., "The Growing Concern Over Business Responsibility," California Management Review, 2 (Summer, 1960), 54-61.

Gilman, Glenn, "The Ethical Dimension of American Management," California Management Review, 7 (Fall, 1964), 45-52.

Johnson, Harold L., "Can the Businessman Apply Christianity?" Harvard Business Review, 35 (September-October, 1957), 68-76.

Levitt, Theodore, "The Dangers of Social Responsibility," Harvard Business Review, 36 (September-October, 1958), 41-50.

Lynch, John J., S. J., "Morals in Business," Catholic Mind, 61 (September, 1963), 21-6.

McMurray, Robert N., "Conflicts in Human Values," Harvard Business Review, 41 (May-June, 1963), 130-45.

Miller, Sammuel H., "The Tangle of Ethics," Harvard Business Review, 38 (January-February, 1960), 59-62.

Niebuhr, Reinhold, "The Cultural Crisis of Our Age," Harvard Business Review, 32 (January-February, 1954), 33-8.

Norris, Louis W., "The Moral Hazards of the Executive," Harvard Business Review, 38 (September-October, 1960), 72-9.

Nossiter, Bernard, "The Troubled Conscience of American Business," Harper's Magazine, 227 (September, 1963), 37-43.

O'Donnell, Cyril J., "The Source of Managerial Authority," Political Science Quarterly, 67 (December, 1952), 573-88.

Oliver, Henry M., "Trends Toward a New Moral Philosophy For Business," Business Horizons, 1 (Spring, 1958), 33-43.

Pettitt, Thomas A., "Management Ideology—Myth and Reality," California Management Review, 3 (Winter, 1961), 95-102.

Smith, Richard Austin, "The Incredible Electrical Conspiracy," Fortune, 63 (April and May, 1961), 132 ff. ; 161 ff.

Votaw, Dow, "What Do We Believe About Power?" California Management Review, 8 (Summer, 1966), 71-88.

Worthy, James, "Religion and its Role in the World of Business," Journal of Business, 31 (October, 1958), 293-303.

Zebot, Cyril A., "Ethos Patterns in a Competitive Society," Review of Social Economy, 15 (March, 1957), 1-25.